Dyeing in Plastic Bags

No mess –
No fuss –
Just great colours!

Helen Deighan

Acknowledgements

In August 2000, having fractured my right wrist and unable to do anything except type, rather slowly, with my left hand, I embarked on writing the book I had been planning for years.
At that time I was blissfully unaware of the trials and tribulations that lay ahead. But, with the help and encouragement of friends, colleagues and family, we made it – and I dedicate this book to them all.

Thanks in particular go to my daughter Emma, who encouraged me to actually start, and my husband, Michael, for his unremitting faith in me. Thanks also to my friend Marie, who managed to keep the house in some sort of order, my colleagues for their support, the students at Treloars for the loan of their tee shirts, Dinah Travis and Pat Salt for agreeing to write the foreword, and Rainbow Silks for the dye to make the samples.

Many thanks to Thérèse Tobin for her patience in trying to make sense of my ramblings and Philip Chambers for his wonderful photography.

My special thanks to Toni Goffe for the illustrations which, with his humour and talent, brought the book alive.

Lastly and by no means least my special thanks to Janet McCallum for her professionalism as a book designer, her inspiration as a textile artist and her care and understanding as a good friend.

Dyeing in Plastic Bags

ISBN 0-9540333-1-0

© Helen Deighan 2001

Illustrations by © Toni Goffe 2001
Telephone 01420 84483

Photography by Philip Chambers
Telephone 01483 481078
annandphil@yahoo.com

Designed by Janet McCallum

Edited by Thérèse Tobin

The rights of Helen Deighan and Toni Goffe to be identified as the author and illustrator of this Work have been asserted by them in accordance with the Copyright, Designs and Patents Act 1988.

First published in Great Britain 2001, 2nd edition 2001, New Edition 2002
Wiro Bound Version also available

10 9 8 7 6 5 4 3 2 1

Published by Crossways Patch
Rose Glen, Crossways Road, Grayshott, Hindhead, Surrey GU26 6HG

Telephone +44 (0) 1428 605554
www.crosswayspath.co.uk

A CIP record is registered by and held at the British Library.

Contents

Foreword

We first met Helen demonstrating her exciting methods of dyeing with simple household equipment working on a trestle table in a busy exhibition hall and we were immediately drawn to her. She was surrounded by buckets of water and plastic bags filled with brilliant colours and fabrics visibly reacting to their various potions.

Helen showed us how her unique way of dyeing fabric would work in a domestic situation. We were struck by the value this marvellous method of colouring would be to the quilter, showing how the apprehension one has of the science of dyeing could be eliminated. Our own kitchens could survive the onslaught of dyeing a large range of colours and tones without undue mess and disruption. It works! We have done it under Helen's expert step-by-step instructions with no trouble at all, and followed that up by taking it into the classroom with great success.

We continue to meet Helen demonstrating, each time with a new idea, for instance making use of the lowly cat-litter tray. These ideas and more have now all come together in this long-awaited book of serious work with light-hearted overtones, making the whole business of dyeing such irresistible fun.

Pat Salt and Dinah Travis

Pat Salt and Dinah Travis are probably best known for bringing quiltmaking into education. They also ran the pilot scheme for both parts of the City & Guilds Patchwork and Quilting, and designed the first distance learning programme for the courses. They are practising quiltmakers interested in advancing the craft in new ways and exhibit both nationally and internationally.

Introduction

I caught the textiles bug at an early age. My mother told me that one of my favourite toys as a very young child was a tape measure – winding it up and then seeing the patterns you could make by pushing it up in the middle to create a tower. I loved fabric and was fascinated with things like knitting and couldn't wait to learn. I won my first national competition at the age of seven with a knitted hot-water-bottle cover.

I was first taught patchwork by an elderly aunt using hexagons and paper, and I must say I did find it all rather tedious and slow. So I moved on to other things and it wasn't until the early 80s that I discovered the joys and excitement of machine patchwork.

Armed with the only book I could find – Beth Gutcheon's 'The Perfect Patchwork Primer' – I taught myself the rudiments of this fascinating craft.

It was not long before I started experimenting with dyeing my own fabrics – initially boiling up great vats of colour and then turning to cold-water dyes, but still in buckets.

I was continually disappointed as the colours I was getting were not the bright vibrant examples I had envisaged. When I looked carefully, I realised that the only bright strong fabrics were those that went into the dye first. I tried mixing colours again, but this time I used a fresh dye bath for each piece of fabric.

What a difference – each piece came out as I wanted, some even better that I had imagined.

It was about this time that one of my patchwork students, after seeing the results I was getting, asked me to take a dyeing workshop. I started to plan and soon realised that if I had 10 students who were all going to dye at least 10 different pieces of fabric, there were going to be a lot of bowls around. The thought of this taking place in the domestic science room at the local school filled me with horror. I would have to come up with a more suitable container.

That night just happened to be 'Take away curry' night and while I was unpacking the food, I saw the portion of salad in a plastic bag. This got me thinking: if a bag like that could hold a pint of water, then it could be used as a container for the dye. I couldn't wait to try. I abandoned my curry and started hunting for plastic bags. The family thought I had gone quite mad as the rest of the evening was spent filling bags with water and testing them for strength.

The workshop was a huge success and everyone was surprised at how easy and clean this method of dyeing was. I then went on to develop the technique and, in 1990, I produced the first booklet – 'How to dye in a plastic bag' – the title of which has brought a smile to many a face over the years.

I have now decided it is time to put all the techniques together in a book, along with some ideas for taking things further and some storage ideas.

All the methods explained are very simple and straightforward, and use readily available equipment and materials.

My philosophy has always been 'if I can achieve what I want simply, why get complicated?' and I apply the same to my dyeing techniques.

Have fun, and remember – mistakes can always be over dyed.

Before you start

Covered in this chapter

■ A word about colour
Dyes and safety
Fabric
Getting the solutions ready
Measurements

■ A word about colour

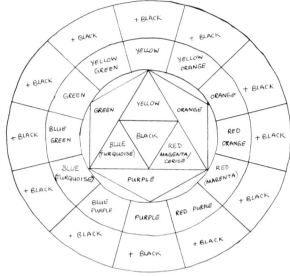

Colour is one of those things that is so important but that so many people seem to find difficult. 'I am no good with colour' is something I hear time and again at workshops. If you can get the colour right, then the finished piece is going to look good; unfortunately, the converse is also true.

I do not intend to pursue the subject of colour theory in any great depth at this stage as there are some very good books on the market should you wish to take it further.

- The Elements of Color – *Itten*
- Blue and Yellow don't make Green – *Wilcox*
- Colour – *Zelanski and Fisher*

More details of these books can be found in the Book list on page 78.

Suffice it to say that a basic understanding of the colour wheel is useful when you begin to dye your own fabrics. See facing page and above.

As you can see, there are three primary colours, red, blue and yellow. When these are mixed, they produce secondary colours – purple, green and orange – which can be mixed again with a primary colour to produce tertiary colours: blue-green, yellow-green, blue-purple, red-purple, yellow-orange and red-orange. The last bit of theory is that if colours are mixed with their complement, the one lying opposite on the colour wheel, a grey is produced.

It is useful to be aware of this theory to know that when the three primaries get together, colours can start to get a bit sludgy. If you want your colours to stay clear and bright, just stick with two primaries. If you have ever seen a young child painting, you will know that it doesn't take long for that lovely bright creation to turn into a sea of mud!

Mixing your own colours has some very positive advantages:

- Firstly, one of cost: it is not necessary to invest in vast numbers of different colours of dye.
- Secondly, and perhaps more importantly, the colours you mix will all 'go' together beautifully because they contain the same source colours. A major problem of patchwork solved.

! Tips – overdyeing

This is the process by which fabric that has already been dyed is dyed again. It can be very useful when the dyeing process has gone wrong, or the results are not what were wanted. Some points to remember:

- Any fabric can be overdyed, even commercially dyed and printed fabrics.
- Different effects can be created by retying a piece in a different direction – see Chapter 4.
- Colours can be mixed – you cannot make a dark colour lighter but it can certainly be changed.

'Colour Wheel' 115cm x 115cm – based on the twelve-part colour circle that appears in Johanne Itten's book 'The Elements of Colour'. See the diagram on the facing page.

Fabrics in the outer circle all had black added to the dye mixture and the fabrics in the border were all produced from the three primary dyes and black.

'Square Peg'
(below) 87cm x 87cm
Made from hand-dyed fabric and black cotton.
Machine pieced, hand quilted.

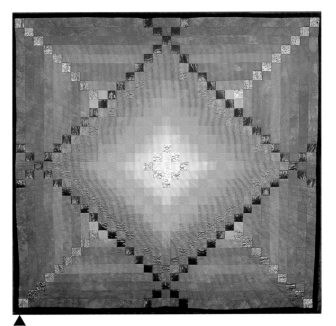

'Shepherds Delight'
(above) 176cm x 176cm
Made from hand-dyed fabrics with some lamés and satins.
Machine pieced and quilted.
Used by Association Française du Patchwork to advertise an exhibition held in SW France 1993.

Hand-dyed fabric –
using magenta, turquoise, yellow and black Procion dyes.

'What goes on in there?' (above)
115cm x 115cm
Made from hand-dyed fabrics with some lamés and satins.
Machine pieced, hand quilted.
Winner of Quilt Art Trophy – Great British Quilt Festival, Harrogate 1991.

'Vasarely 1' 125cm x 125cm (above right)
Made from hand-dyed fabric and black cotton.
Machine pieced and quilted.

'Refracted Rainbow' (right)107cm x 94cm
Made from hand-dyed fabric.
Machine pieced and quilted.

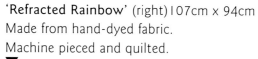

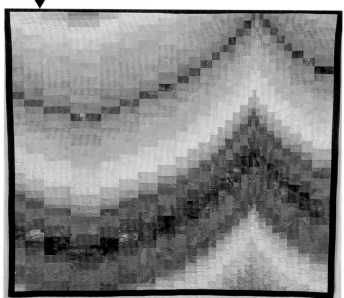

'Piccalilli' 132cm x 132cm
Made from hand-dyed fabric and dark blue cotton.
Machine pieced, machine quilted / embroidered.
Winner of Advanced Category and Trophy for best geometric quilt in National Quilt Championships, Ascot 2000.

▪Dyes and safety

Choosing your dyes

The dyes I would recommend are good quality, pure colour, fibre reactive dyes. I use Procion MX dyes and these are becoming increasingly easy to obtain. Mail order addresses can be found at the back of the book.

In their book on colour, Zelanski and Fisher say that, although in theory it may be true that all other colours can be mixed from only the three primaries and black, in reality this is only possible when using printer's inks and in colour photography.

It was for this reason that I first selected magenta, turquoise and lemon yellow as my dye colours as, together with a black dye and the white of the fabric, it is possible to mix a vast number of hues, shades, tints and tones. The colours mentioned are all pure and cannot be made by mixing other colours. It is important that the dyes you are using are pure colours so that the mixing is under your control.

A simple way to determine if an MX dye is pure is to carefully sprinkle a tiny amount of the dye powder on the surface of some cold water in a white dish. It is quite easy then to see if the dye is pure, consisting of just one colour, or if it is a mixture of colours because, as the grains separate on the surface of the water, different colours can be easily identified.

You will see, for example, that a red could be made up of magenta and yellow (two of the three 'primary' colours). If this red were then mixed with a blue, the result would be a brown rather than the purple you were expecting. This is because of the presence of some yellow, the third primary colour.

In conclusion, to start dyeing you only need to buy four dye powders in the following colours:

- Turquoise
- Magenta, Cerise, Brilliant Pink or Fuchsia
- Lemon or Citrus Yellow
- Black

The names can vary depending on the supplier.

Safety precautions

1 It is advisable to wear a dust mask and have adequate ventilation when handling dyes in powder form.
2 Wear rubber gloves and protect work surfaces.
3 Always keep dye, dust and dirty hands away from your eyes.
4 Keep dye and any utensils used away from food.
5 Containers and utensils used in dyeing should be kept separate from food preparation equipment.
6 When working with children, always mix the dye into solution beforehand and remember that children should be supervised at all times.

▗Fabric

Choice of fabric

Use 100% cotton to achieve the best results. It is possible to use a polyester/ cotton mix but the result will be paler as only the cotton fibres will take the dye.

It can be hard to determine the fibre content of fabric, and I don't always believe retailers who say a piece is 100% cotton! There are two simple tests. One is to crease a piece of the fabric with your thumbnail; cotton will give a really good crease whereas the polycotton will not.

Another test that gives really well defined results is to cut a small piece of the fabric and burn it. If it burns with a white smoke and the residue is a fine powder that feels like talcum powder when rubbed between your fingers, then the fabric is cotton. If, however, it burns with a black smoke and the residue is sticky or hard and gritty, the fabric has got a percentage of man-made fibres in it and will not take the dye as well.

Check labels of tee shirts: they should say what the garment is made from.

There is of course a wide range of cotton fabrics on the market. On the chart opposite you can see the results of some tests I did on some readily available fabrics. When it comes down to it, however, it is what you can easily get hold of... For my part, I use cotton sheeting. It comes in 150 cm (60 in) wide pieces and takes the dye well. English calico and American muslin are also good. In fact, I really like the look of rough calico when it is dyed, as the rather matt finish gives the illusion of suede and can look fantastic.

Beware treated fabrics such as chintz and some lawns, as the treatment can affect the way the cloth handles the dye.

Fabric preparation

Washing

Whichever fabric you have, it must be washed before use, particularly English calico as it does contain lots of dressing. I usually wash all my fabric in 3 metre pieces as I buy them, and store them like this ready for dyeing, when time, enthusiasm and space allows it.

Cutting

Cut pre-washed fabric into suitably sized pieces. As a quilt maker, one of the reasons I dye my own fabrics is to produce a wide range of colours in smallish pieces. I find squares of about 50 cm x 50 cm (20 in x 20 in) the best to fulfill my needs. For those of you familiar with patchwork terms, about the size of a 'fat quarter'. If, however, you want long strips, cut metre (yard) pieces of fabric selvage to selvage.

Marking

Before dyeing begins, each piece of fabric can be marked with an identification number. Then as you dye each piece, write down in a note-book the recipe used with the fabric number. Although this involves a bit more work, it does make it easier to sort out a load of freshly dyed pieces of fabric. I use a laundry marker to mark the fabric – the thin felt-tip variety works well.

Fabric chart

Fabric	Overall colour	Even dye	Scrunch effect	Suitability for patchwork
George Weil cotton CC150 Bl	Good	Good	Quite good	Good
Whaleys medium calico CC37	Not bad – a bit yellow	Quite good	Fair	Good
Whaleys mercerised cotton CM13	Very good – bright and strong	Good	Very good	A bit heavy
Whaleys calico AJ404 scoured (shrunk)	Quite good – a bit yellow	Quite good	Fair	Good
Whaleys chintz cotton white CM1S 459	Quite good – a bit yellow	OK	Poor	Fair – bit limp
Whaleys cotton lawn CD18	Very good	Very good	Good	A bit too fine for patchwork
Whaleys fine bleached cotton CD10	Good	Good	Quite good	Very limp – frays easily
Whaleys plain cotton CD11	Fair	Poor	Good	Good
Whaleys scollata cotton natural CD69B	Strong but a bit yellow	Not bad	Fair	A bit limp
Whaleys scoured cotton natural CP10	Quite good – a bit yellow	Fair	Quite good	Good
Whaleys WB1582 cotton (shrunk)	Fair – a bit pale	Fair	Quite good	Good
Polycotton	Poor	Pale but even	Poor	Poor
Linen / viscose mix	Good, strong colour	Quite good	Quite good	Poor – frays easily
Linen – natural colour	Very good	Quite good	Quite good	Poor – frays easily
Cotton velvet	Good	Good	Interesting	Difficult
Polyester	Very poor – no real colour	Unsuitable		
Cotton curtain lining – white	Quite good	Quite good	Fair	Too limp – frays easily

Fabrics were all cut to the same size and dyed in separate plastic bags in
Procion dye solution – turquoise and black ratio 4:1.

Getting the solutions ready

Salt

Reason for use
Salt is the agent for driving the dye out of the water and into the fabric. Although the dyes used in this book will react without the use of salt, the resulting colours will not be as strong. It should be noted that the less water you use, the less salt is required.

Availability
I use bags of salt I can buy cheaply at the supermarket. Nothing special, in fact the cheaper the better.

Making up solutions
Measure out 500 gm (2 cups) of salt. If you intend doing a lot of dyeing, try and find a container of some sort that you can use as a measure in the future. I discovered that a pot that contained a certain brand of flavoured instant noodles was just the correct size for this amount of salt. This meant all I had to do next time round was pour out a pot-full and I knew I had the correct amount. To my palate, the noodles were revolting but the pot was great!

Dissolve the salt in 2 litres (8 cups) of very hot water. Stir until all the salt has completely dissolved and then pour into a suitable container for storage. I find that large laundry-liquid bottles fit the bill very well. Allow to cool before using.

This solution will last for months if not contaminated with soda solution.

Soda

Reason for use
Fibre reactive dyes will only react when the PH value is high – i.e. very alkaline. Soda crystals raise this PH value, therefore when it is present with the dye, in water, it quickly causes the dye to react. If it were not there, the dyes would not react and a permanent bond with the fabric would not take place.

Soda is a fixing agent and should not be confused with a mordant, which is used in other types of dyeing, particularly natural dyeing.

Availability
The actual crystals are sodium carbonate and I find the washing soda I buy in the supermarkets in the UK is fine. Just beware that things such as bleach can sometimes be added to this product and I would not recommend the use of such brands. The bleach would work against the dye and your results would be disappointing. Check the packet and, if there is no indication of additives, then it is OK to use. I have to say that I have been buying and using washing soda for years and it has always worked well for me. Alternatively use soda ash bought from your dye retailer – or, apparently, it is possible to use the sodium carbonate used in swimming pools but I have not tried it so am unable to give an opinion.

! Be careful!
Take care not to mix up the bottle caps of the soda and salt solutions as this can cause contamination.

Making up solutions

The soda is mixed in the same way as the salt. Measure 400 gm (2 cups) and mix with 2 litres (8 cups) of hot water; when dissolved, store in a suitable container. And guess what? The noodle container used to measure 500 gm of salt takes 400 gm of soda crystals. How's that for a bit of luck! If using soda ash, you will only require 80 gm (5 tablespoons) to make 2 litres of solution.

Dye

Mixing

The dye powder is sometimes quite difficult to mix and, if the particles are not completely dissolved, you will not get an even dye. Sometimes this can give unexpected and rather interesting results. If, however, you want to start with a well-mixed solution, I suggest the use of a little hand whisk – the sort that has a coil of wire in a half-moon shape. I got one as a free gift from a mail-order company and it has proved to be invaluable. If you want stronger colours, experiment by adding more dye powder.

Add a little squirt of washing-up liquid to the dye solution – this helps the dye powder to blend more readily with the water.

Avoiding hazards

The dye is bought as a powder and it is in this form that it can be a health hazard. The powder is very fine and can be inhaled if care is not taken. The danger then is that this can cause an allergic reaction and, horror of horrors, could prevent you from dyeing in the future. So please be careful. I would advise the use of a mask, just at this stage. Once the dye is in a solution, the main danger has passed.

It is for this reason that I would always advise mixing the dye solutions first before you start any dyeing, and then put the lids back on the containers and put them away.

If you intend to do any dyeing with children, always make up the solutions on your own before the session begins. Whenever I take a workshop, I try and do this; it saves a great deal of anguish and unnecessary fuss.

Pure dye solution recipe

Dissolve 1 teaspoon of dye powder in 100 ml (⅓ cup) of tepid (not hot) water. This will give you about 10 dessertspoons. You will be able to calculate how many dessertspoons you will need, and therefore how much dye solution to prepare, when you have read through the different 'dyeing process' instructions. See pages 14, 24, 28 and 54.

At this stage, keep the colours separate and pure. It helps if each jar has its own dessertspoon for measuring out, then there is no chance of the colours getting mixed. It is amazing what the tiniest drip of turquoise can do to a whole jar of yellow.

I put 4 jars, containing my four pure dye solutions, together in something like an ice-cream container. This is just an added precaution against the risk of spilling.

> ### Tips
> It is worth noting at this point that in order to get a really good dye reaction, the dye bath temperature should be just about room temperature. So, when mixing the dye baths, use water that is cold to tepid. It is not essential, and don't get too worried about it, but it is worth knowing that a dye bath that is either too hot or too cold will not react as well.
> - A dye bath that is too hot will react too quickly, and have little effect on the fabric.
> - A dye bath that is too cold will react too slowly to be effective.

■Measurements

Easy ways to measure

These days, with the use of different units of measurement, measuring is becoming increasingly complicated and confusing.

Firstly, let me say something about the need for precise measuring when you are doing the sort of dyeing covered in this book. There is *no* need!

When you are dyeing natural fibres, such as cotton, it is very difficult to get exact repeat dyes – the only reason for accurate measuring, in my opinion. The sort of factors that can affect the dye are things such as the weather (hot, cold, humid or dry), the type of water used (hard or soft), the weave of the fabric, the quality of the cotton used – even the weather on the day the cotton was picked can have an effect. All these factors are really out of our control and, if we are not going to be working under laboratory conditions, why bother to measure like chemists?

I find the easiest way to overcome the problem of measuring out reasonably accurate amounts is to find my own measuring containers.

Some examples:
- The instant-noodle pot that was the right size for 500 gm of salt and 400 gm of soda crystals. To start with, I weighed out the salt using scales and then poured it into different containers until I found one that was just about right.

- The same with 100 ml of solution. I measured out this amount using a measuring jug then poured the liquid into the caps of different laundry-liquid bottles until I found a suitable one. It is also easy to mark jars with some coloured plastic sticky tape with the measurements you are going to need. I just find it so much easier to fill to the red mark, for instance, than squinting to see those little numbers each time.

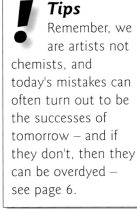

Tips
Remember, we are artists not chemists, and today's mistakes can often turn out to be the successes of tomorrow – and if they don't, then they can be overdyed – see page 6.

Measurements used in this book

Metric measurements have been used in this book with the equivalent cup measurement given in brackets.

The cup size is the US version, which is approximately 240 ml.
As there is no convenient measure in cups for 100 ml, I have suggested ⅓ cup is used. I can assure you that this does work – I have tried both. For the scientists among us, if cup measurements are used throughout, the soda and salt solutions will come out slightly stronger, therefore less is required in the dyeing recipes.

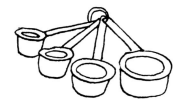

The dessertspoon measure used is approximately 10 ml and is used because you easily buy packs of plastic picnic spoons which are the right size – i.e. larger than a teaspoon (5 ml) and smaller than a serving spoon (15 ml). Quite honestly, the way I am suggesting you dye in this book is not exact and the odd 10 ml is neither here nor there – just relax and have fun.
If you are using cup measurements, do so throughout – and the same applies to metric measurements. By far the easiest method is to find containers as described above and then you can forget all about millilitres and cups and get on with the serious business of colouring cloth.

Plastic-bag dyeing

2

Covered in this chapter

- Equipment and materials
- The dyeing process
- Dyeing times
- Mixing colours

▮ Equipment and materials

You will need

1 1 litre (2 pint) bowl
2 Cling film
3 A measuring jug or jar marked with the required amount
4 Rubber gloves, old clothes, protected surfaces, etc.
5 Cat-litter trays – see below
6 Plastic bags – see below
7 Pure dye solutions – see page 11
8 Soda solution – see page 10
9 Salt solution – see page 10
10 Fabric pieces approximately 50 cm x 50 cm (fat quarters) – see page 8

! Safety note
Remember to keep utensils used for this purpose separate from those used for food preparation.

Plastic bags

You are going to need some good quality, strong freezer bags – either medium or large – the sort you can buy in the supermarket for freezing vegetables, etc. I still use the old style bags and just tie a knot to make them secure. I did have a go with the zip-lock kind of bag but I didn't like them as much. There are not, of course, any hard-and-fast rules on this and you use the bags you like the best.

The size needs to be about 30 cm x 40 cm (12 in x 16 in)

This is a rough guide. I usually buy a packet of large bags but have used the medium size ones as well.

Cat-litter trays

I use cat-litter trays to hold the bags once they are filled with dye. A good sized one will take about 8 bags and then there are no worries about leaks or whatever. Any tray or large plastic container, such as an old washing-up bowl, would also do for this purpose.

▪The dyeing process

1 Get ready

Have everything that you are going to need ready.
Then put an open plastic bag into the bowl.

2 Make up the dye bath

Into the bag put:

- 5 dessertspoons of pure dye solution

- 100 ml (⅓ cup) of soda solution

- 100 ml (⅓ cup) of salt solution

- 500 ml (2 cups) of cold water

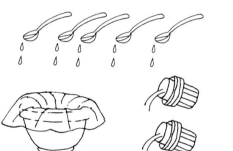

> **! Tips**
> As soon as you mix soda, salt and a fibre-reactive dye together, the reaction will start to take place and the dye will only remain active for 3 – 4 hours. Also, it will be at its most active when it is first mixed with the soda. So get the fabric into the solution now and don't decide to go and have a cup of tea – go immediately on to the next stage, then have a break.

3 In goes the fabric

Now, very carefully into this mixture put your prepared fabric.

If you want an evenly dyed piece, wet the fabric first; if you want it a little bit mottled, put it in dry and don't agitate so much.

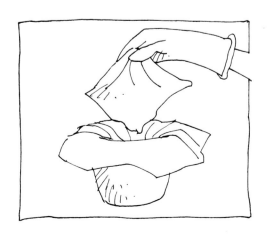

4 Push the fabric down

Push the fabric into the dye – you can do this without touching the dye if you keep your hand on the outside of the bag.

Pull up the top of the bag and gently twist to close. Holding the top of the bag in one hand, then keeping your other hand on the outside of the bag, carefully push the fabric into the dye – in this way you do not touch the dye and you stay clean. That's the theory, anyway!

5 Check for leaks

Gently lift the bag out of the bowl and check for leaks. If you see anything untoward, take the whole bowl to a sink and either transfer dye and fabric into another bag, or just lift the leaking bag and put it and its contents into another bag. I can go for ages without any leaks and then, for no apparent reason, I will have a couple – and it usually happens when I am demonstrating.

6 Tie a knot

If all is well, tie a firm knot in the top of the bag, trying to exclude as much air as possible. The more air you get out, the less room there is for the fabric to come out of the dye.

7 Agitate and leave

Remove the bag from the bowl and gently agitate for about five minutes to make sure the fabric is evenly dyed.

Put the bag to one side in a cat-litter tray or something of the kind. Make sure the top of the bag is sticking up. If it is bent over, you will find dye solution will begin to seep out.

Leave the bag for at least an hour, two to three if possible, agitating from time to time.

 **Tips**
Remember, the more you agitate, the more evenly dyed your fabric will be – as well as doing wonders for stress relief!

> **Tips**
> During the time that the bag is left, you can continue dyeing other pieces of fabric following steps 1 – 7. Now you can start mixing the pure colours. Ideas for recipes can be seen on page 19 in the 'Mixing Colours' section.
> Just remember, 5 spoons of dye in total each time.

Dyeing times

You have two choices: you can either leave the bag for an hour or leave it for 3 or more – see below for details.

Leaving for one hour

This way gives you the opportunity of dyeing more pieces of fabric in the same dye bath.

- Go back to the bag after an hour, put it back into the bowl.

- Carefully untie the knot and remove the fabric. Squeeze out as much of the solution as you can and wrap the fabric in a piece of cling film. Leave this in a tray and wash and rinse when ready.
  It is a good idea to leave the fabric like this, overnight if possible, to give the dye time to set.

- Go back to the bag and put another piece of fabric into the same solution. This will give you a paler version of the first piece.
  This method works well when using pure colours. However, when the colours are mixed, the pigment comes out of the dye at different rates and the colour as well as the tone will change. A purple will become quite blue.

- You can try putting in another piece of fabric after a further hour – but remember, the dye will only remain active for 3 hours.

Leaving for three or more hours

This will give the dye longer to react with the fabric, which will give a stronger colour. When dyeing cotton, it suits me to leave the bags standing overnight. I would not do this, however, if I were dyeing silk, as the soda can have an adverse effect on the silk fibres.

Leave the bag for 3 hours or longer. The dye is then spent and can be thrown away.

- Take the bag to a sink or a large empty bucket. Carefully expose one of the bottom corners and either pierce the plastic or snip off the corner. Make sure you do this while the bag is supported in another vessel and the corner has been pulled away from the dye solution, otherwise, as you make a hole, you will create a beautiful coloured fountain.

- Gently allow the dye solution to drain away. When the bag is empty of dye, it is possible to squeeze the fabric through the bag and remain clean.

- Wrap the top of the bag round the main body of the bag that contains the fabric and leave this little bundle in a tray until you are ready to rinse and wash it.

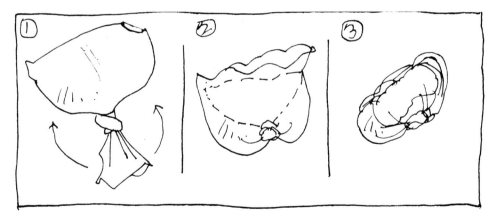

- Again, it is a good idea to leave the fabric like this, overnight if possible, to give the dye time to set.

Washing and rinsing

For washing, rinsing and drying your fabric, follow the instructions that can be found in Chapter 6, page 48.

 Tips
Leaving the fabric to set allows the dye time to thoroughly soak into the fabric and make a permanent bond with the fibres. Although not essential to the dyeing process, stronger, deeper colours will be achieved if time is allowed for this to take place.

■Mixing colours

Why mix?

When you start mixing colours, just remember the rules of the colour wheel. See page 6.

If you want bright vibrant colours, stick to two primaries.

If you want colours that are a bit sludgy, then start gradually to introduce either the third primary or black. See page 20.

As I said before, the joy of mixing colours from just three pure colours is that everything you produce will 'go' together. I find this one of the wonderful bonuses of dyeing my own fabrics. Just take a look at the collection of fabrics opposite page 6. These were all produced from just three primaries and black.

How to mix

The plastic-bag-method of dyeing has been used, with the following recipes, to produce fabrics suitable for patchwork. A range of greens, for example, can look great when put together in a quilt.

Instructions for dyeing can be found on the following pages:

- plastic-bag dyeing – page 14

- fabric preparation – page 8

Should you require larger pieces of fabric, the amounts in the recipes can be increased as long as the ratio remains the same.

For example:

- 3 turquoise + 2 yellow, would become 6 turquoise + 4 yellow, or 9 turquoise + 6 yellow

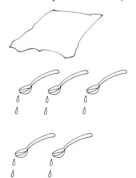 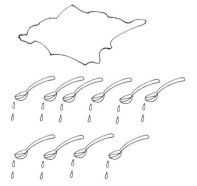 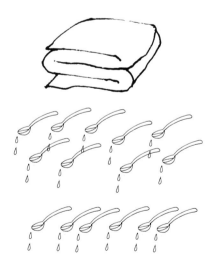

Mixing with primary colours

To get a range of greens, follow the recipes shown opposite.

All you have to do is look at recipe number 1, put this number of dessertspoons of dye into the bag along with the soda solution, salt solution and water.
Then take fabric number 1, wet it and put it into the bag.
Then go on to recipe number 2 and fabric number 2.

Recipes for greens

Bright colours:

Number 1   5 dessertspoons of turquoise
Number 2   4 dessertspoons of turquoise + 1 dessertspoon of yellow
Number 3   3 dessertspoons of turquoise + 2 dessertspoons of yellow
Number 4   2 dessertspoons of turquoise + 3 dessertspoons of yellow
Number 5   1 dessertspoon of turquoise + 4 dessertspoons of yellow
Number 6   ½ dessertspoon of turquoise + 4 ½ dessertspoons of yellow
Number 7   Drip of turquoise + 5 dessertspoons of yellow
Number 8   5 dessertspoons of yellow

By adding black, some interesting sludgy colours can be made.

Number 9   5 dessertspoons of turquoise + 1 dessertspoon of black
Number 10   4 dessertspoons of turquoise + 1 dessertspoon of yellow + 1 dessertspoon of black
Number 11   3 dessertspoons of turquoise + 2 dessertspoons of yellow + 1 dessertspoon of black
Number 12   2 dessertspoons of turquoise + 3 dessertspoons of yellow + 1 dessertspoon of black
Number 13   1 dessertspoon of turquoise + 4 dessertspoons of yellow + 1 dessertspoon of black
Number 14   ½ dessertspoon of turquoise + 4 ½ dessertspoons of yellow + 1 dessertspoon of black
Number 15   Drip of turquoise + 5 dessertspoons of yellow + 1 dessertspoon of black
Number 16   5 dessertspoons of yellow + 1 dessertspoon of black

Carry on dyeing

Carry on with the orange range and the purple range. If you have already got fabric dyed using 5 yellow or 5 turquoise, there is obviously no need to repeat them in the other ranges – just adjust the numbers accordingly.

I have used cerise for these recipes, but equally good results can be obtained with the use of a magenta dye or a fuchsia dye.

> **! Tips**
> If you want the fabrics to be as evenly dyed as possible, remember to agitate – 5 minutes at the start then from time to time during the 3 hours.

Recipes for oranges

Bright colours:

Number 1   5 dessertspoons of cerise
Number 2   4 dessertspoons of cerise + 1 dessertspoon of yellow
Number 3   3 dessertspoons of cerise + 2 dessertspoons of yellow
Number 4   2 dessertspoons of cerise + 3 dessertspoons of yellow
Number 5   1 dessertspoon of cerise + 4 dessertspoons of yellow
Number 6   ½ dessertspoon of cerise + 4 ½ dessertspoons of yellow
Number 7   Drip of cerise + 5 dessertspoons of yellow
Number 8   5 dessertspoons of yellow

By adding black, some interesting sludgy colours can be made.

Number 9   5 dessertspoons of cerise + 1 dessertspoon of black
Number 10   4 dessertspoons of cerise + 1 dessertspoon of yellow + 1 dessertspoon of black
Number 11   3 dessertspoons of cerise + 2 dessertspoons of yellow + 1 dessertspoon of black
Number 12   2 dessertspoons of cerise + 3 dessertspoons of yellow + 1 dessertspoon of black
Number 13   1 dessertspoon of cerise + 4 dessertspoons of yellow + 1 dessertspoon of black
Number 14   ½ dessertspoon of cerise + 4 ½ dessertspoons of yellow +1 dessertspoon of black
Number 15   Drip of cerise + 5 dessertspoons of yellow + 1 dessertspoon of black
Number 16   5 dessertspoons of yellow + 1 dessertspoon of black

Recipes for purples

Bright colours:

Number 1   5 dessertspoons of cerise
Number 2   4 dessertspoons of cerise + 1 dessertspoon of turquoise
Number 3   3 dessertspoons of cerise + 2 dessertspoons of turquoise
Number 4   2 dessertspoons of cerise + 3 dessertspoons of turquoise
Number 5   1 dessertspoon of cerise + 4 dessertspoons of turquoise
Number 6   5 dessertspoons of turquoise

By adding black, some interesting sludgy colours can be made:

Number7   5 dessertspoons of cerise + 1 dessertspoon of black
Number 8   4 dessertspoons of cerise + 1 dessertspoon of turquoise + 1 dessertspoon of black
Number 9   3 dessertspoons of cerise + 2 dessertspoons of turquoise + 1 dessertspoon of black
Number 10   2 dessertspoons of cerise + 3 dessertspoons of turquoise + 1 dessertspoon of black
Number 11   1 dessertspoon of cerise + 4 dessertspoons of turquoise + 1 dessertspoon of black
Number 12   5 dessertspoons of turquoise + 1 dessertspoon of black

> **! Tips**
>
> You will notice I have included some extra pieces in the orange and green sets. This is because yellow is a pale colour and the effect of a darker colour like turquoise is very marked. You will be surprised how just a drip of turquoise or black can dramatically change the yellow. If, however, you tried a drip of yellow into turquoise, the change would hardly be noticeable.
>
> These recipes are intended as starting points for you to create your own palettes of fabric. Once you get the hang of it, experiment a bit for yourself – and always remember, *mistakes can be over dyed* – see page 6.

Mixing with secondary colours

When two primary colours (red, blue or yellow) are mixed together, a secondary colour is produced, e.g. purple. When this secondary colour is mixed with the third primary colour, muddy browns or greys are produced. This is why it is so important to have true clear primaries if you want to mix bright colours.

If, however, you want a range of interesting colours that are a little more muted, experiment with the recipes on page 21. They also work very well when combined with tie-and-dye techniques.

Select a secondary colour recipe from the first batch of dyeing e.g.

- purple made from 3 dessertspoons of cerise + 2 dessertspoons of turquoise

Into a separate jar, mix 3 times this amount from your original pure dye solutions:

- 3 dessertspoons of cerise x 3 = 9 dessertspoons of cerise
  and 2 dessertspoons of turquoise x 3 = 6 dessertspoons of turquoise

Dye pieces of fabric using the mixed dye and yellow, following the recipes as shown below.

Recipes for purple and yellow mix

Number 1	4 dessertspoons of purple + 1 dessertspoon of yellow
Number 2	3 dessertspoons of purple + 2 dessertspoons of yellow
Number 3	2 dessertspoons of purple + 3 dessertspoons of yellow
Number 4	1 dessertspoon of purple + 4 dessertspoons of yellow
Number 5	½ dessertspoon of purple + 4 ½ dessertspoons of yellow
Number 6	Drip of purple + 5 dessertspoons of yellow

If you carry on like this – first mixing up a secondary colour and then combining it with the third primary – you will be able to mix an enormous number of different shades.

Don't forget that the recipe for the secondary colour can be changed. In fact, you could work your way through the list of purples, then the greens ... are you starting to imagine the possibilities?

> **!** **Tips**
> What about mixing black with these secondary mixes? Have Fun!

Get ready!

Graduated effects

Covered in this chapter

■ Plastic-bag method
■ Dip-dyeing
Other ideas to try

I mentioned in the chapter on plastic-bag dyeing that it is possible to get different depths of an original colour by adding more pieces of fabric after the first one has been removed from the bag. This, however, is not so successful when using mixed colours.

Of course, as always, there is a simple way to overcome the problem, and a range of at least 8 different tones of the same colour can be produced.

> ### ! Safety note
> Remember to keep utensils used for this purpose separate from those used for food preparation.

■ Plastic-bag method

Equipment and materials

You will need

1 1 litre (2 pint) bowl
2 Cling film
3 A measuring jug or jar marked with the required amount
4 Rubber gloves, old clothes, protected surfaces, etc.
5 Cat-litter trays – see page 13
6 Plastic bags – see page 13
7 Pure dye solutions – see page 11
8 Soda solution – see page 10
9 Salt solution – see page 10
10 Fabric – see page 8
11 Extra clean jam jar – see below

Extra jar

You will also need a clean jar marked with a half-way line.
Use a piece of thin, coloured, sticky tape to mark the line as this shows up better than a drawn line.

1 Prepare the dye solution

Into the clean marked jar you are going to put 10 dessertspoons of dye solution.

Mix the colour you want by looking on pages 19 and 20 to find the recipe for your choice of colour using and just double the number of spoons, e.g.

recipe from original list was   3 turquoise + 2 yellow
into the jar, put   6 turquoise + 4 yellow

Then top up the jar with cold water and stir.

2 Get ready

Make sure you have everything you are going to need.

You won't need the container of mixed pure dyes so these can be put away.

Put an open plastic bag into the bowl.

3 Make up the dye bath

Into the bag put:

- half the jar of dye solution

- 100 ml (⅓ cup) soda solution

- 100 ml (⅓ cup) salt solution

- 300 ml (1 cup) cold water

4 In goes the fabric

Carefully put the first piece of fabric into this solution and, when it is completely immersed, tie a knot in the bag, agitate and leave on one side for three hours.

Detailed instructions on how to do this can be found on page 15.

5 Refill the jar of dye

Go back to the jar of dye and top it up again with cold water.

It is now a weaker solution of the same colour.

6 Just carry on dyeing

Now put another open plastic bag into the bowl and repeat steps 3 and 4.

You will find you are able to do this at least 8 times before the dye becomes too weak to use.

7 Time to come out

After 3 hours, the fabric can be removed from the dye solution and left to set for 12 – 24 hours (it depends how impatient you are!).

Detailed instructions on how to do this can be found on page 17.

8 Wash and rinse

Follow instructions for washing, rinsing and drying in Chapter 6, page 48.

! **Tips**
Remember, the more you agitate, the more evenly dyed your fabric will be – as well as doing wonders for stress relief!

▮Dip-dyeing

Sometimes it is good to have a change in the intensity of a colour on one piece of fabric – strong colour one end, gradually getting paler and paler, to white at the other end.

It is quite simple to achieve this but, as you will see from the instructions, you will need to be around for about 3 hours to get the best results.

Dip-dyeing is when a piece of fabric is lowered, bit by bit, into the dye bath. The end of the fabric that goes into to the dye first will be a stronger colour than the end that goes in last. This is because the dye solution will get weaker as more fabric is lowered into it; also the first end will be immersed in the dye for the longest period.

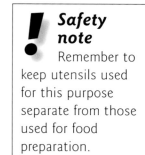

Safety note
Remember to keep utensils used for this purpose separate from those used for food preparation.

Equipment and materials

You will need
1 Plastic box – see below
2 Ruler – see below
3 Sticky tape
4 Measuring jug
5 Rubber gloves, old clothes, protected surfaces, etc.
6 Cling film
8 Fabric – see below
9 Pure dye solutions – see page 11
10 Salt solution – see page 10
11 Soda solution – see page 10

Plastic box
A rectangular plastic box of some sort – 4 litre ice-cream box would be ideal.

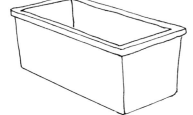

Ruler
A piece of wood or a ruler which is about 5 cm (2 in) wide and which is long enough to rest on the top of the box lengthways.

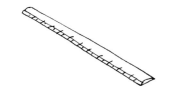

Fabric
The fabric should be prepared and ready to use – see page 8.

For this technique you will need fabric approximately 115 cm x 30 cm (45 in x 12 in).

Or, to put it more simply, a length of fabric that is about the width of your box.

I Attach the fabric

Stick one narrow end of the fabric to the ruler/wood using the sticky tape.

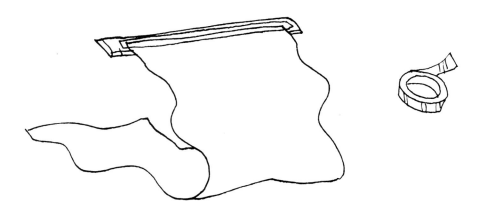

2 Roll up the fabric

Carefully roll up the fabric on to the ruler. Try and keep it as straight as you can.

3 Make up the dye bath

Into the box put:

- 5 dessertspoons of dye solution, mixing the pure dye solutions to get the colour you want, just like you did with the plastic-bag dyeing

- 100ml (⅓ cup) soda solution

- 100ml (⅓ cup) salt solution

- 500ml (2 cups) cold water

4 Get ready

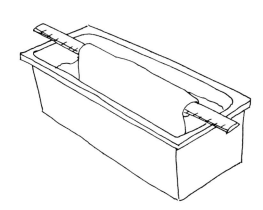

Carefully place the ruler with the fabric wrapped round it on top of the box.

Gently turn the ruler so that the fabric untwists and the end goes into the dye.

Just let about 5 cm (2 in) go into the dye and leave the ruler, with the roll of fabric in place, on top of the box.

5 Carry on twisting

At about 10 – 15 minute intervals, turn the ruler over once – which will let another 5 cm (2 in) of fabric go into the dye.

Carry on like this until you can twist no more – i.e. you have got to the sticky tape.

Leave it like this for another quarter of an hour and you will see the dye creep up the fabric – but you should still be left with a white bit at the top.

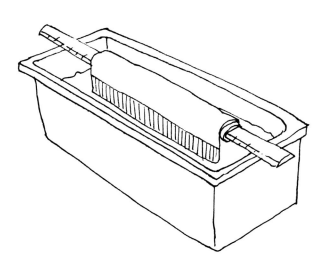

> **Tips**
> So I don't have to keep clock watching, I use the electric timer on the cooker – I set it to 15 minutes and, when it rings, I just give the ruler a turn.
>
> DING !
>
>

6 Take out the fabric

Lay a long piece of cling film on a protected surface – a little longer and wider than the length of fabric.

Then take the white end of the fabric off the ruler and carefully remove the whole length from the dye. Gently squeeze out excess liquid as you lift.

Then lay the fabric on top of the cling film. Fold one end of the cling film over the end of the fabric and continue to fold up like this so that the dyed pieces do not touch each other.

Leave to set for 12 – 24 hours if you can wait that long. It can come out sooner if you want!

7 Wash and rinse

Follow instructions for washing, rinsing and drying your fabric as given in Chapter 6, page 48.

Other ideas to try

▪ Two colours

Dip-dye one piece of fabric using one colour.

After you have finished and the fabric is washed, rinsed and dried, you can repeat the operation using this length of fabric by putting it in another colour, starting at the other end.

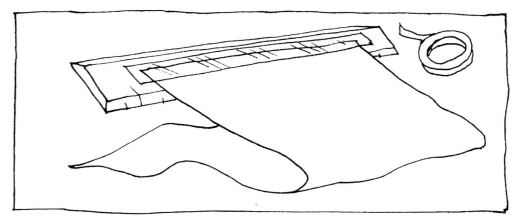

For example, if you dyed a piece turquoise through to white, you could then attach the strong turquoise end to the ruler and start by dipping the white end in a cerise dye.

When you have finished, you will have a length of fabric that is turquoise one end and cerise the other, with all the shades of purple in between. See examples on facing page.

▪ Pleating fabric

Instead of using a length of fabric that is the same width as the box, try with a piece that is wider and pleat it as you stick it to the ruler. This will give you a bit of a tie-dyed effect.

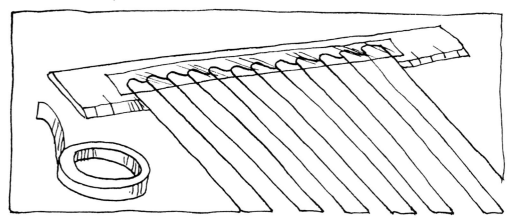

▪ Carry on with your own ideas

As with all the techniques in this book, once you have mastered the basic method, try out some ideas of your own. Nothing is lost, except for a bit of dye and your time – and you might gain a great deal.
Remember, mistakes can be over dyed!

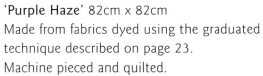

Graduated strips dyed using the ruler technique described on page 26.

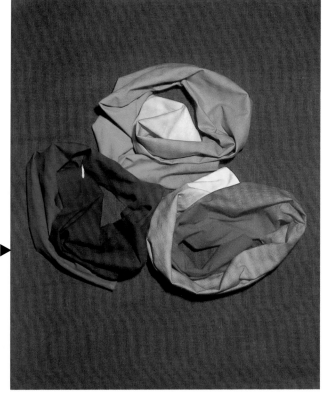

'Purple Haze' 82cm x 82cm
Made from fabrics dyed using the graduated technique described on page 23.
Machine pieced and quilted.

'Spring Greens' 82cm x 82cm
Made from hand-dyed fabric.
Machine pieced and quilted.

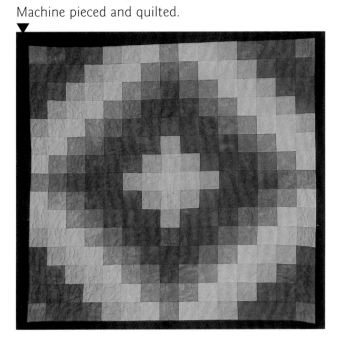

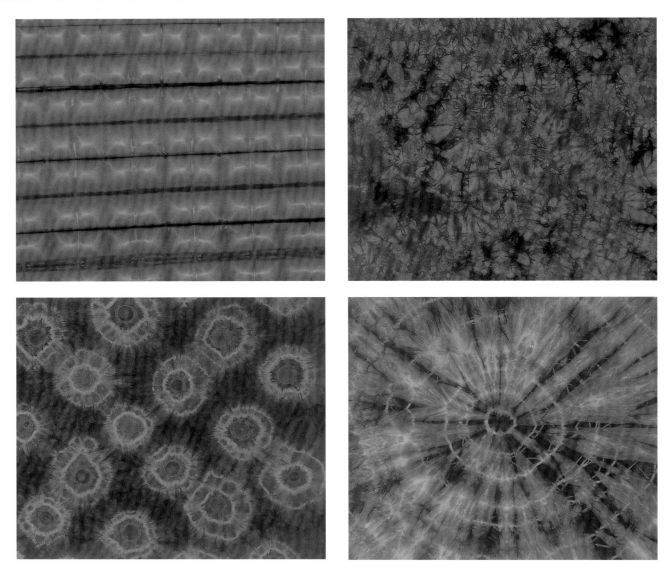

Examples of tie-and-dye
techniques described in
Chapter 4, page 31.
Folded (top left)
Scrunching (top right)
Circles (middle left)
Sunburst (middle right)
Tying round a drainpipe
(right)

Tie-and-dye techniques

Covered in this chapter

Equipment and materials
Folded techniques
Scrunching
Circles
Sunburst
Tying round a drainpipe
Dyeing the tied pieces

Interesting effects can be obtained by tying, folding, knotting and scrunching fabric before it is dyed.

This technique of resist dyeing has been used for hundreds of years by people throughout the world to decorate cloth.

Examples can be found in India, Africa, South America and Japan, as well as ideas of our own from the 60s – I remember them well!

I will explain just a few basic techniques which I hope will give you some idea of the process. You can then either develop other ideas for yourself or research the subject further – there are some very good books around on the subject, which I am sure you will find interesting.

▮Equipment and materials

You will need

1 Elastic bands
2 String or strong cotton thread
3 Old tights or stockings
4 A piece of drainpipe or a large plastic bottle
5 An iron – normal domestic (steam or dry)
6 Fabric – see below

> **! Tips**
> If wet fabric is used for tye-and-dye, the water will act as an additional resist leaving larger white areas. Dry fabric allows the dye to seep in, giving for me, more interesting results.

Fabric

Fabric should be prepared and ready to use – see page 8.

Cut the fabric into suitably sized pieces.

Because the pieces will be tied up, it is possible to dye slightly larger pieces than with the basic plastic-bag method.

Folded techniques

1 Pleat in one direction

Lay the fabric out flat and pleat up one side.

Carry on until the whole piece has been pleated

2 Pleat in the other direction

Now start pleating in the other direction, concertina fashion, until you have a little parcel.

> **! Tips**
>
> For really sharp lines, iron down each fold as you go.

3 Make secure

Secure the parcel with string or elastic bands.

> **! Tips**
> It can be very effective if the fabric is first folded, tied and then dyed in one colour and then, after untying, washing and drying, it is re-folded in the opposite direction and then dyed in a contrasting colour.

Examples can be found facing page 31.

Scrunching

This is not just the easiest technique, but it is also one of the most effective.

▪ Using elastic bands or string

1   Take a piece of fabric and hold it by one corner with your left hand.

2   Then with your right hand, start to pick up small pieces, twist them and then gather them up into your left hand.

Left-handers – reverse hands.

3   When all is safely gathered in, secure with an elastic band or string to make a ball.

▪ Using an old stocking or a pair of tights

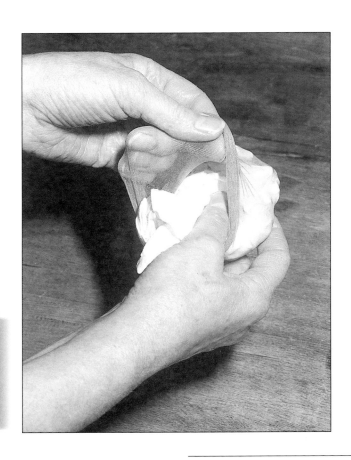

1   Cut the foot off an old, reasonably fine, stocking.

2   Instead of pinching, twisting and gathering in your hand, pinch, twist and push the fabric into a stocking.

3   When all is in, tie a knot in the stocking to form a ball.

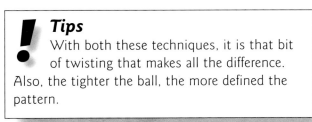

! Tips
With both these techniques, it is that bit of twisting that makes all the difference. Also, the tighter the ball, the more defined the pattern.

■Circles

Small circles can be made on a piece of fabric with this method. It can be quite fiddly and time-consuming, but the results are worth it.

1 Mark out

If you want your circles to be evenly distributed on the fabric, you must mark the spots before you start. It is very difficult to see once you begin tying up.

On a plain piece of fabric, mark out where you want the circles to be. Use a pencil – something that will wash out during the dyeing process.

2 Start tying

You can either use small pebbles or buttons and tie these into the fabric, using string or elastic bands. Or you can just pinch a small piece of the fabric and tie round it.

Examples can be found facing page 31.

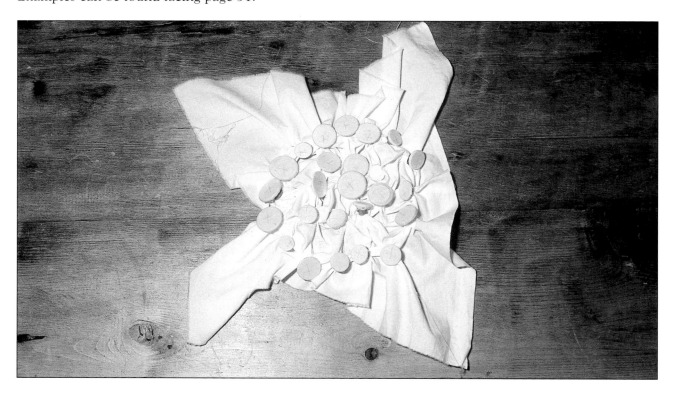

Sunburst

This is a traditional tie-and-dye technique and examples can be seen all over the world.

1 Start in the middle

Use a square of fabric and pinch up a piece in the centre, letting the rest fall down in pleats.

2 Tie it up

Begin at the point and bind the fabric with string. Do a few rounds in one place then move down a couple of cms and do a few more rounds. Pull the string tight and knot it off before moving down to the next round.

> **! Tips**
> Try and keep the fabric pleated for best effect.
> One way of doing this is to iron the fabric in half, then in half again in the opposite direction, being careful not to iron over the first crease. Do the same on the diagonals. This will make a star shape and, because of the creases, the fabric will fall into pleats more easily.

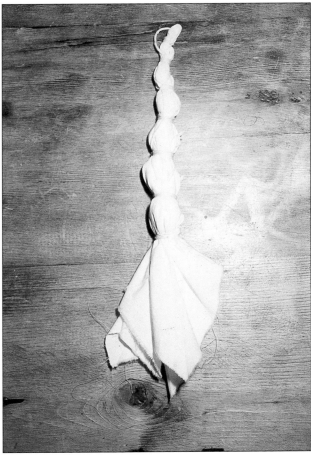

Tying round a drainpipe

This can give some interesting effects, particularly when the fabric is pleated up around the pipe.

A plastic 10 cm (4 in) drainpipe is ideal. A piece about 30 cm (12 in) long is enough. Or you could use a large plastic bottle.

You will need a piece of fabric wide enough to go comfortably round the circumference of the pipe, and as long as you want.

1 Wrap around

Take the piece of fabric, wrap the narrow end round the pipe and secure with a strong elastic band.

2 Carry on down the pipe

About 6 cm (2½ in) down the pipe, put another elastic band over the fabric. Then push this one up to lie next to the first one. As you do this, the fabric will be scrunched up.

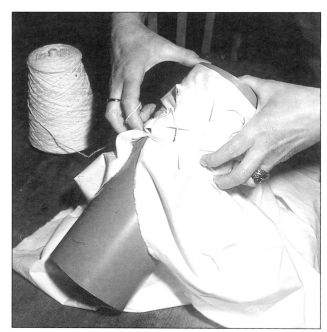

3 Keep on going

Carry on adding elastic bands and scrunching up the fabric until all the fabric is on the pipe.

 Tips
- String or tape can be used, instead of elastic bands. Use whichever you find the easiest.
- The technique can be varied in the way the fabric is attached to the pipe and scrunched up.
- It can be twisted, pleated, twisted first one way and then the other, etc.
- A large plastic bottle could be used if you don't have a drain pipe.

▪Dyeing the tied pieces

With the exception of the pipe-wound pieces, all the tied techniques can be dyed in a plastic bag. Just make up the dye bath as you would for normal plastic-bag dyeing and put in the tied-up pieces. Because these do not need as much space, I usually put two or three in the same bag.

Excluding the air

Make sure you get as much air out as you can – you will see it is more difficult to submerge tied up fabric, particularly the sunburst one!

No need to agitate

Once you are sure all the pieces are in the dye, there is no need to agitate – you are not wanting evenly dyed samples this time. Put the bag on one side and leave for the required time – see page 17, plastic-bag dyeing.

I do go back to the bags from time to time and just turn them to make sure there are no pieces sticking out.

Pipe-wound fabric

I will explain two ways to dye the pipe-wound fabric and you may well think of a third.

1   Lay the covered pipe in a tray of dye-bath solution (i.e. dye, soda and salt solutions + water) and turn gently.

    Do this until all the fabric is soaked with dye – leave, turning the pipe every 20 minutes or so to make sure the dye solution has really soaked in. After 2 hours, remove and wrap in cling film to set.

2   Lay the covered pipe in a tray and pour over the mixed dye-bath solution – the good thing about doing it this way is that you can use more than one colour. Leave, remove and wrap as in the first method.

Untying

When to untie? That is a frequently asked question and there is not really a hard-and-fast rule, but this is the way I do it.

Once the fabric has been left to set, I take it out of the cling film and rinse it well in cold water. (This gets rid of most of the dye so you don't get in such a mess when you start to untie the pieces.)

I then undo the string or remove the elastic bands or whatever, rinse again and then carry on with the normal washing, rinsing and drying routine.

> **! Tips**
> Beautiful effects can be achieved by re-dyeing fabric in a contrasting colour. When the fabric is dry, it can be re-tied either using the same technique but in a different direction or using a completely different technique, before being dyed in another colour.

Cat-litter-tray dyeing

5

Covered in this chapter

Equipment and materials
First method – the soda is added after the dye and the salt
Second method – the soda is added along with the salt and the dye
Third method – the soda is added to the fabric before dyeing begins

This technique, known as space dyeing, is a really good way of creating interesting effects quite quickly. Also, because you can see where the dye is going, it allows for a bit more control than with the total immersion dyeing methods.

I shall describe three different methods, which will produce differing results. See examples facing page 52. In each method it is the time at which the soda solution is added, that creates the different effects.

- Method 1 – the soda is added after the dye and the salt

- Method 2 – the soda is added along with the salt and the dye

- Method 3 – the soda is added to the fabric before dyeing begins

Have a go, see what happens and, as always, once you are familiar with the basic technique, start to experiment.

The only rules to remember are:

- Natural fibres work best, such as cotton, silk or linen.

- The dye must be left on the fabric long enough to work.

- Soda must be added at some point to fix the dye.

▪Equipment and materials

You will need

1 Cat-litter-trays or something similar
2 Cling film
3 Rubber gloves, old clothes, protected surfaces, etc.
4 Measuring spoons
5 Dessertspoons and jars for dye solution
6 Fabric – prepared and ready to use – see page 8
7 Soda solution – see page 10
8 Salt solution – see page 10
9 Dye powder

▪First method

This method gives a more muted effect, with the colours blending into one another.

I Make the dye solution

Mix ½ teaspoon of dye powder in a jar with:

- 50 ml (¼ cup) of salt solution

- 250 ml (1 cup) water

- a squirt of washing-up liquid to help the dye powder to mix

Mix until the dye powder has completely dissolved. Any particles left will show up as dark splodges on the fabric – can be effective if this is what you want!

> **! Tips**
> You can vary the amount of dye powder to get either stronger or lighter colours. More dye powder for stronger colours and less for paler shades.

Mix up 3 separate colours like this, or 4 if you want to include black.

To begin, I suggest you use the 3 primaries used for the other techniques – i.e. Turquoise, Magenta and Lemon Yellow.

2 Fabric into the tray

Put a piece or pieces of fabric into the tray.

The fabric can be scrunched up or folded in a variety of ways.

A good technique is to lay out the fabric as flat as possible and then pinch little pieces and twist them to make little spiral effects in the fabric. Do this at intervals all over the fabric.

The fabric can be used wet or dry. Dye will not run as much on dry fabric as it will on wet. Experiment to find the technique you like the best.

Spoon over the dye solutions, mixing the colours as you do so.

3 Blend the colours

To get the colours to blend, gently press the fabric with the back of your hand or squeeze it, and you will see the colours mixing – but do be aware of mud! (See Tips below)

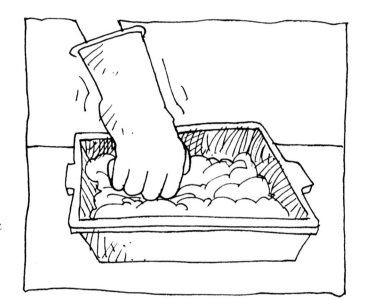

! Tips

Be careful when you are using the three primaries as they can get very muddy when they mix. There are a couple of things you can do to try and avoid the brown marks that appear when the colours all mix together at the bottom of the tray.

- First – tip away any excess liquid straight away before it gets a chance to stain the fabric.
- Second – just use two primary colours and, when the fabric has been dyed, rinsed, washed and dried, begin the whole process again using the third colour. You will still get brown where the 3 colours meet, but you will have more control as the first two colours will be stable.

4 Leave to penetrate

Leave the fabric in the tray so the dye can really get into the fibres and react. You can carry on gently moving the fabric to get the colours to blend, or you can just leave it to do its own thing.

Leave for 5 – 10 minutes

5 Add soda solution

Mix 100 ml (⅓ cup) of soda solution with 500 ml (2 cups) of water and pour this over the fabric.

Leave for 30 minutes.

6 Tip away

Tip away all the dye liquid and wash and rinse the fabric – see Chapter 6, page 48 for details.

Alternatively, the fabric can be wrapped in cling film until you are ready to wash it.

See Second method, page 44, for details.

7 Wash and rinse

See page Chapter 6, page 48, for instructions on washing and rinsing.

Second method

This method gives a more dramatic effect than the first method, with the colours staying more separate and vibrant.

1 Make the dye solution

Mix ½ teaspoon of dye powder in a jar with:

- 50 ml (¼ cup) of salt solution

- 100 ml (⅓ cup) of soda solution

- 100 ml (⅓ cup) water

- a squirt of washing-up liquid to help the dye powder to mix

Mix until the dye powder has completely dissolved. Any particles left will show up as dark splodges on the fabric – can be effective if this is what you want!

Mix up 2 or 3 colours like this – 4 if you want to include black.

> **!** **Tips**
> Remember that as soon as dye, salt and soda are mixed, a chemical reaction will start and the dye will begin to deteriorate. It will take at least 3 hours before it is useless, but only employ this method if you intend to use up the dye solution, otherwise it will be wasted.
> Also, wait until the last minute to prepare the dye solution.
> Have everything else ready first.

2 Fabric into the tray

As with the first method, put a piece of fabric into the tray, scrunching up the fabric as you do so – see First method, page 40.

The fabric can be used wet or dry. Dye will not run as much on dry fabric as it will on wet. With this technique, the colours will remain really vibrant when dry fabric is used.

Spoon over the dye solutions. The colours will mix as one dye is spooned on top of another.

! Tips
You can vary the amount of dye powder to get either stronger or lighter colours. More dye powder for stronger colours and less for paler shades.

3 Blend the colours

To get the colours to blend, gently press the fabric with the back of your hand or squeeze it, and you will see the colours mixing – but do be aware of mud!

See Tips in First method, page 40.

4 Leave to penetrate

Leave the fabric for at least 30 minutes so the dye can really get into the fibres.

5 Wrap in cling film

Take a piece of cling film, a bit longer than the fabric, and lay it out on a flat surface.

Carefully pick up the fabric, squeeze out any excess liquid and lay it on the cling film, which should be a bit longer than the fabric. Fold the extra cling film over the fabric, then start to roll or fold up the fabric. The reason for the cling film is to prevent any bits of fabric touching, which will leave marks where you don't want them.

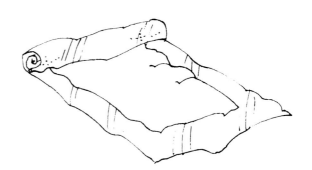

Leave the fabric wrapped in cling film overnight or until you are ready to rinse and wash.

By doing this, the dye will be stronger, and there always seems to be less to wash out – which is a bit of a bonus.

6 Wash and rinse

See Chapter 6, page 48, for instructions on washing and rinsing.

 **Tips**
Remember to wash the tray carefully before returning it to the cat – or better still, buy one of your own!

Third method

This method gives quite a dramatic effect, and you don't need to worry about the dye solution deteriorating as the dye powder is only mixed with water.

1 Make the dye solution

Mix ½ teaspoon (see Tips on page 39) of dye powder in a jar with:

- 250 ml (1cup) of water

- a squirt of washing-up liquid to help the dye powder to mix

This makes quite a strong solution. Should you want slightly paler shades, mix with more water.

Mix up 2 or 3 colours like this – 4 if you want to include black.

2 Prepare the fabric

With this method the fabric is soaked in a solution of soda and salt before dyeing begins.

In a jug, mix up the following :

- 500 ml (2 cups) water

- 100 ml (⅓ cup) soda solution

- 100 ml (⅓ cup) salt solution

Put dry, washed fabric in a bowl and pour over the soda and salt mixture. Leave to soak for 30 minutes. Wring out the fabric and dry.

> **! Tips**
> Watch the weather if you are drying the soaked fabric outside. A sudden shower could wash out the solution and you would have to soak it all over again.

3 Fabric into the tray

As with the first method, put a piece of fabric into the tray, scrunching up the fabric as you do so – see First method, page 40.

In this method, as with the others, the fabric can be used wet or dry. But do not dip the fabric in water to wet it; instead, just sprinkle on some water while it is in the tray. This ensures that no solution is washed away.

Spoon over the dye solutions, mixing the colours as you do so.

4 Blend the colours

To get the colours to blend, gently press the fabric with the back of your hand or squeeze it, and you will see the colours mixing – but do be aware of mud!

> **! Tips**
>
> Be careful when you are using the three primaries as they can get very muddy when they mix. There are a couple of things you can do to try and avoid the brown marks that appear when the colours all mix together at the bottom of the tray.
>
> - First – tip away any excess liquid straight away before it gets a chance to stain the fabric.
> - Second – just use two primary colours and, when the fabric has been dyed, rinsed, washed and dried, begin the whole process again using the third colour. You will still get brown where the 3 colours meet, but you will have more control as the first two colours will be stable.

5 Leave to penetrate

Leave the fabric for at least 30 minutes so the dye can really get into the fibres.

6 Wrap in cling film

Take a piece of cling film, a bit longer than the fabric and lay it out on a flat surface.

Carefully pick up the fabric, squeeze out any excess liquid and lay it on the cling film which should be a bit longer than the fabric. Fold the extra cling film over the fabric, then start to roll or fold up the fabric. The reason for the cling film is to prevent any bits of fabric touching, which will leave marks where you don't want them.

Leave the fabric wrapped in cling film overnight or until you are ready to rinse and wash.

By doing this, the dye will be stronger, and there always seems to be less to wash out – which is a bit of a bonus.

7 Wash and rinse

See Chapter 6, page 48, for instructions on washing and rinsing.

! Tips
Any of these cat-litter-tray methods can be used to dye large pieces of fabric for backing quilts, etc.

Use the largest tray you can find – ones made for large cats – and I have found a piece of fabric 1.5 metres by 3 metres is a useful size.

Final stages 6

Covered in this chapter

- Washing and rinsing
- Drying and ironing
- Checking for fastness
- Rectifying problems

Washing and rinsing

It is most important that any fabric that has been dyed by any of the methods described should be washed and rinsed thoroughly.

Fibre-reactive dye, as its name suggests, works by chemically reacting with the fibres in a fabric. Any dye that has not reacted is left and must be washed away to avoid any 'bleeding' problems.

1 Cold rinse

First, rinse fabric in cold water. Do this by hand and keep all colours separate.

Fabrics can very easily contaminate each other when they are allowed to touch at this stage.

2 Hot wash

Next, wash fabric in hot soapy water. Again, I do this by hand and keep all colours separate.

I use a good quality, eco-friendly laundry liquid for this purpose.

At this stage it will look as though all the dye is being washed away and you will be left with white fabric. Do not worry. This is the excess dye that must be discharged so that the fabric will be wash-fast.

> **! Tips**
> I have found that doing the rinsing and washing this way is good for getting your hands clean, should you have forgotten to don your rubber gloves while doing the dyeing.

3 Hand rinse

After the hot wash, rinse the pieces of fabric in cold water again, until the water runs clear. Red always seems to take longer than other colours, but take heart, it will run clear in the end.

4 Final rinse

If I have had a big dyeing session, I put all the fabrics together in the washing machine for one final rinse and spin.

Drying and ironing

Drying

I have found that dye seems to be more stable once it has been dried. It is for this reason that I try and get it dry as quickly as possible. This can be done outside, but not in direct sunlight; it is best to do it inside, on a clothes horse or in a tumble drier.

Ironing

I always think dyed fabric looks so much better once it has been ironed. I still get a thrill looking at a pile of beautifully dyed, freshly ironed fabrics.

My offspring may call me sad, but my pleasures are simple.

> **! Tips**
> It is much easier to iron fabric that is slightly damp.

■Checking for fastness

If the washing and rinsing procedure has been completed correctly, you should have no problems with colours running or bleeding.

If, however, you are not totally convinced of this, there are a couple of tests you can do. This is perhaps particularly important if the item you intend making will be regularly washed, for instance a cot quilt or a baby jacket.

Tests

Washing

Cut some strips of dyed fabric and white fabric.

Sew these together, alternating colour and white.

Wash this sample in hot soapy water, rinse and check for stains.

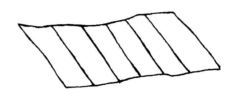

Ironing

Put a piece of white fabric on the ironing table. Iron a piece of damp, dyed fabric on top of this and check for stains.

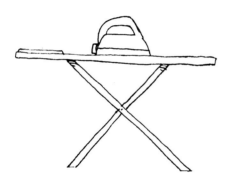

Washing Machine

A piece of white fabric could be put in the washing machine when the dyed pieces have their final rinse. If this comes out white, the dye is fast.

Rectifying problems

If, for some reason, the colours continue to run, or you have bought some fabric you are not sure about, there are a few things you can try.

- Repeat the whole washing and rinsing process. There is a product called Synthrapol (see List of suppliers, page 77) which is good for troublesome colours. It is used instead of laundry liquid.

- Repeat just the rinsing process, adding some salt solution to the rinse water.

> **! Tips**
> Use Synthrapol sparingly. Just a teaspoon will do as it does produce a lot of foam. Do not use in front-loading washing machies. Other products are Metapex 38 liquid and Fixitol – see Glossary, page 79.

If all else fails, there is a product on the market that looks like a piece of cloth. This goes in the washing machine when the article containing a troublesome fabric is washed. This product is called a Laundry Magnet and can be bought from specialist suppliers, see page 77. I don't know how it works, but somehow it attracts any rogue bits of dye and stops the colours from running. Colour Catchers work in much the same way and are sold in packs of 10 and can be bought in any good supermarket.

> **! Tips**
> While on the subject of fastness, fibre-reactive dyes produce colours which are light fast. This does not mean that if the fabric is left in full sun for months on end, the colours will not fade – but under normal conditions, the colours will remain true for years. Which is more than can be said for some commercially dyed fabrics.
>
> If you are washing something made with a mixture of hand-dyed fabrics, e.g. a patchwork cot quilt, the trick is to get it dry immediately after washing, preferably in a tumble drier. The risk of colours running is increased when fabric is allowed to remain wet for any length of time.

Dyeing with children

Covered in this chapter

▪ Introduction
▪ Tie-and-dye tee shirts
▪ Space-dyed tee shirts

▪ Introduction

Children really enjoy participating in dyeing projects but it can be quite nerve wracking when buckets of permanent dyes are involved. A bit of careful planning, good organisation and getting things ready before the event, however, can make the occasion enjoyable for all.

I have found that the plastic-bag technique works well. Some bags may spring a few leaks due to over enthusiastic agitating, but other than that, I have experienced no major disasters.

Before the session begins

1   Mix all dyes required with water and put away pots of dye powder. It is essential that this is done without help from the children.

2   Protect surfaces with plastic sheeting – stick down edges with tape.

3   Have buckets of water at each table – the less the children have to move about, the better.

4   Wash all tee shirts to be dyed.

5   It is useful to have some examples of work to show.

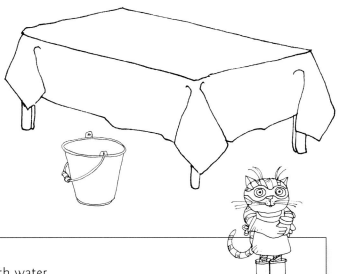

Safety note
- ▪ Have all dyes to be used already mixed with water.
- ▪ No tasting, licking fingers or rubbing eyes with dyed fingers.
- ▪ Make sure there is plenty of room to work – accidents can happen when people are too cramped.
- ▪ Protect all work surfaces and floor if precious.
- ▪ Old clothes to be worn.
- ▪ Make sure children have all they need to hand, to avoid unnecessary wandering about.
- ▪ Have plenty of mopping up cloths to hand in case required.

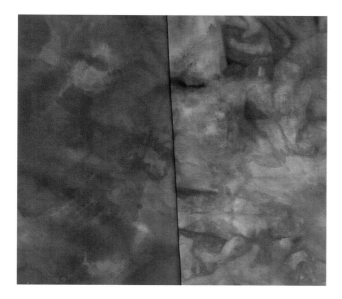

Examples of fabric dyed using the techniques described in Chapter 5, page 38, Cat-litter-tray dyeing.

Method 1 – the soda is added after the dye and the salt (left).

Method 2 – the soda is added along with the salt and the dye (below left).

Method 3 – the soda is added to the fabric before dyeing begins (below right).

In each of these three photographs, the fabric on the left was made wet before dyeing commenced and the fabric on the right was dry.

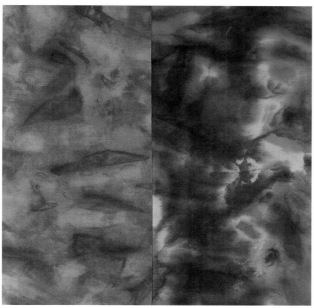

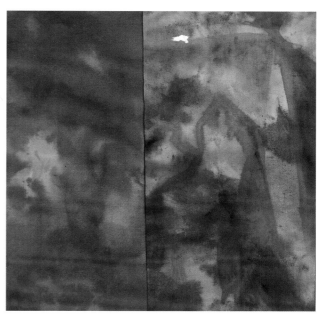

'Two Worlds' 135cm x 206cm. Made from fabrics dyed using the graduated technique described on page 23. Commissioned by Treloars, a college for disabled students in Alton, Hampshire, UK, to hang in their chapel. Machine pieced and quilted. ▼

Pushing down the fabric - see page 40 ▼

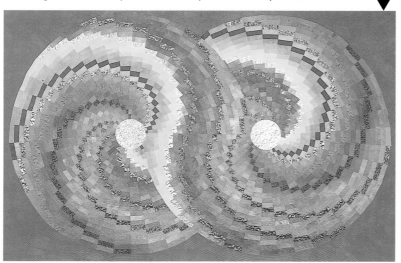

Examples of tee shirts dyed using
different techniques.
Folded tie-and-dye (top left)
Cat-litter-tray dyeing (top right)
Sunburst tie-and-dye (middle above)
Circles tie-and-dye (right)
Scrunching tie-and-dye (below)
See Chapter 7, page 52

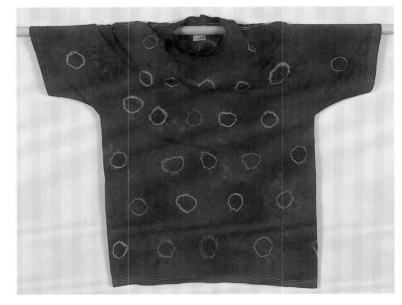

Tie-and-dye tee shirts – plastic-bag method

Equipment and materials

You will need

1 1 litre (2 pint) bowl
2 Cling film
3 A measuring jug or jar marked with the required amount
4 Rubber gloves, old clothes, protected surfaces, etc.
5 Cat-litter trays – see page 13
6 Plastic bags – see page 13
7 Pure dye solutions – see page 11
8 Soda solution – see page 10
9 Salt solution – see page 10
10 Tee shirts – see below

Tee shirts

Make sure the tee shirts to be used are white, that they are made from 100% cotton and that they have all been washed and dried.

Tying

Demonstrate different tying techniques. All the ways described in this book work well with children.

If possible, it is a good idea to have some examples to show the patterns produced by the different techniques.

Set children on to tying their tee shirts.

Dyeing

Demonstrate the basic plastic-bag technique – emphasise the safety rules.

Make sure each child has the following:

- a bowl

- a plastic bag

- a cat-litter tray

Make sure each table has:

- soda solution

- salt solution

- a bucket of water

- a jug

Children can then start to dye their tee shirt.

Basic recipe for an average-sized tee shirt

- 10 dessertspoons of dye solution

- 250 ml (1 cup) soda solution

- 100 ml (⅓ cup) salt solution

- 500 ml (2 cups) water

Depending on the age of the children, it is up to you if you allow them to spoon in the dye. With young ones, I usually do this for them – they, of course, select the colours.

They can then add salt, soda and water. Then they tie a knot and agitate.

It is a good idea to have the bags supported in trays while the agitating takes place, to cope with unexpected leaks.

Because this is tie-and-dye, agitating is not that necessary, but children do enjoy it.

Leave the bags for 3 hours.

Setting, washing and rinsing

Drain the dye out of the bags – take the bag to a sink and carefully cut one corner, let the dye solution drain away, squeezing the tee shirt to get as much out as possible.

Wrap the tee shirt in cling film and leave to set for 24 hours.

Remove from the cling film and, while it is still tied up, rinse the tee shirt in cold water.

Untie the shirt and have a look at the results.

The tee shirt must now be washed in hot soapy water, rinsed in cold water until the water is clear, and then hung up to dry.

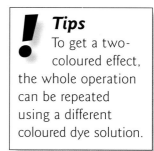

! Tips
To get a two-coloured effect, the whole operation can be repeated using a different coloured dye solution.

Space-dyed tee shirts

Prepare as you did for the previous session, with a few variations.

Equipment and materials

You will need

1 Cat-litter trays or something similar
2 Cling film
3 Rubber gloves, old clothes, protected surfaces, etc.
4 Measuring spoons
5 Jars for mixing dye solution
6 Tee shirts – prepared and ready to use – see below
7 Soda solution – see page 10
8 Salt solution – see page 10
9 Dye powder

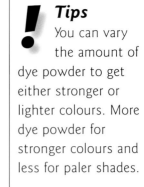

> **! Tips**
> You can vary the amount of dye powder to get either stronger or lighter colours. More dye powder for stronger colours and less for paler shades.

Tee shirts

As well as being washed, the tee shirts will also have to be soaked in a soda and salt solution before the session begins.

Mix up a solution using the recipe below – this will be sufficient for 2 or 3 shirts:

- 500 ml (2 cups) water

- 100 ml (⅓ cup) soda solution

- 100 ml (⅓ cup) salt solution

Put dry, washed, tee shirts in a bowl and pour over the soda and salt mixture. Leave to soak for 30 minutes. Wring out and dry.

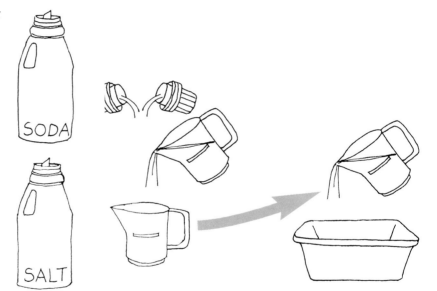

Dye solution

Mix ½ teaspoon of dye powder in a jam jar with:

- 250 ml (1 cup) of water

- a squirt of washing-up liquid to help the dye powder to mix

The strength of the dye solution can be increased, or decreased, by adding more, or less, dye powder.

Make up 2 or 3 colours in this way.

This should be sufficient for 2 tee shirts, but a lot depends on the enthusiasm of the participants.

Pour the solution into washing-up-liquid bottles. This makes it easier for the children to apply the dye.

I half fill the bottles and have plenty of dye solution ready mixed for when the bottles need replenishing.

Dyeing in a tray

Demonstrate this technique and again, if possible, have some examples to show before the children begin.

Scrunch up tee shirt in the cat-litter tray and gently squirt on the colours.

The shirts can be dampened to make scrunching easier and to encourage the colours to run into each other.

Squeezing and moving the fabric about a bit can blend the colours a little.

When there is enough dye in the tray, place tray inside an old plastic carrier bag and leave for at least an hour.

The tee shirts must now be rinsed in cold water, washed in hot soapy water, rinsed in cold water until the water is clear, and then hung up to dry.

> **! Tips**
> In your demonstration, make sure you emphasise the importance of not squeezing the bottle until it is facing downwards into the tray.

Dyeing on a plastic sheet

This is the same technique as dyeing in a tray, but this time it is on a plastic sheet.

Requirements are the same, except that you will need some sort of plastic sheet (see below), and you won't need the cat-litter trays.

This method is best done on the ground.

Spread some plastic sheets on the ground – one for each child. A slit and opened dustbin liner is ideal. Weight down the corners.

Tee shirts can be spread out over the plastic. They will lie better if they are slightly damp.

Colours can be squirted on to the tee shirts and, as they are flat, it is easier to create patterns.

Spirals and spots can look very effective.

Demonstrate this technique and again, if possible, have some examples to show before the children begin.

When the dyeing is complete, cover the shirt with some more plastic and leave. If space is needed, carefully roll up and put somewhere safe.

In either case, leave for at least an hour.

The tee shirts must now be rinsed in cold water, washed in hot soapy water, rinsed in cold water until the water is clear, and then hung up to dry.

! Tips
Do not let the children use too much dye solution – only as much as the fabric will absorb.

Keeping records and storage

Covered in this chapter

- Record book
- Sample book
- More records
- Hanging storage unit

Although it is quite difficult to get exact repeat dyes, it is a good idea to keep a record of your recipes for future reference.

Whichever method of recording you choose, you must make sure you note down the recipe at the time of dyeing and that your fabric is marked with the appropriate number.

Record book

You will need either a book with card or strong paper pages, or some pieces of card which can be hole-punched and kept in a loose-leaf folder.

Cut a small piece of fabric, about 4 x 4 cm, stick this to the card and write down the recipe.

> **!** *Tips*
> Remember to leave each remaining piece of fabric with its number intact, so it can still be matched with the correct recipe at a later date.

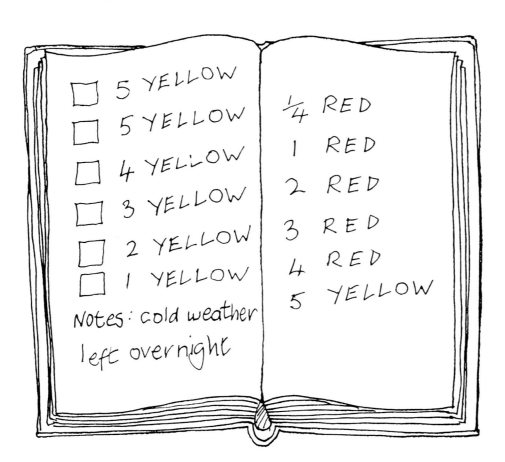

Sample book

A sample book does take a little longer to produce, but I think it is well worth the effort.

I Prepare the samples

Cut samples of fabric about 20 x 10 cm – the size is not crucial, but do try and keep them all the same.

You must keep a check on the numbers of these samples – believe me, it is very easy to get in a muddle.

What I usually do is cut up some scraps of paper and use these to pin a number to each fabric sample as I cut it.

Three edges of the samples should be neatened if your sample book is to last. By far the easiest way is on an overlocker. If that is not possible, a simple zig-zag on the machine is fine, or a small hem.

2 Prepare the pages

Sort the samples into sets, e.g. all the greens.

Take a piece of light-weight card about 30 x 10 cm and fold it in half lengthways.

Arrange the sample pieces along the inside of the fold, overlapping a bit.

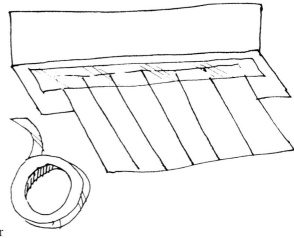

Stick in place using some sticky tape.

Refold the card, covering the raw edges and sticky tape, then sew along the edge. Use a strong needle (number 90) and remember to change the needle when you have finished, as it will not be much good for sewing fabric after this.

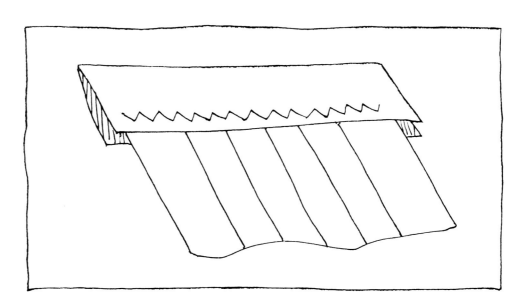

3 Write on recipes

On the top of each piece of card, you need to write the corresponding recipes.

With the first book I made, I printed the recipes onto the card prior to cutting and folding it. This went well – until I realised that the fabric samples were not in the right place for the recipes.

Something to think about before you start to print.

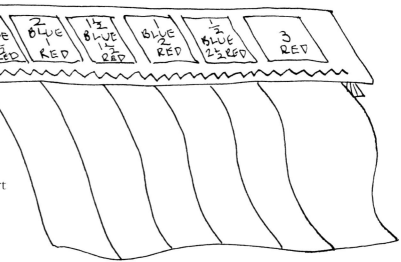

4 Put it all together

Punch and reinforce some holes in the card and then, using hinged metal rings, join the pages to make the book.

More records

As well as the recipes used, you might like to include other information in your record book for future reference.

Information that might prove useful:

- date of dyeing

- length of time left in the dye bath

- length of time left to set

- weather conditions

- type of fabric

All these factors can affect the final result and should be taken into account when repeat dyes are needed.

It is also quite interesting to look back and see just what it was that helped you achieve that fantastic colour.

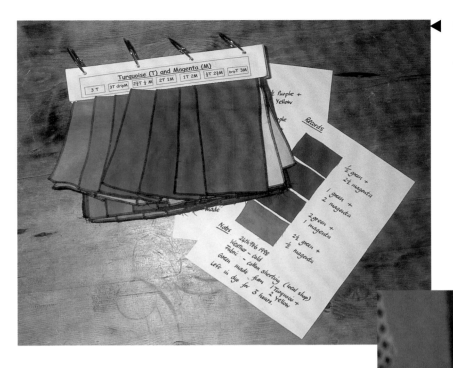

Sample book and record sheets – instructions on how to make these are given on pages 59 – 61.

Threads dyed using various techniques described in this book – see page 70.

Couching – see page 73

Storage unit in use – see page 63

'Cot quilt' – 50cm x 75cm
Made from hand-dyed fabrics and calico.
Machine pieced and machine embroidered.
This quilt was made for my first grandchild who,
at the time of going to press, is still eagerly
awaited.

▼

Hanging storage unit

I store all my small pieces of fabric in a hanging unit similar to the one pictured below.

All the pieces of fabric, no matter how small, can be seen, making selection much easier than rummaging around in a large box or basket.

Mine hangs on a wall away from direct sunlight and I have had no problems with fabric fading.

The unit was made from medium-weight calico. This was used double for extra strength and to create envelopes into which card could be slid to make the base of each section firm.

The unit pictured below has 35 sections, each one measuring about 6 in(15 cm) x 8 in (20 cm) x 6 in (15 cm).

See facing page for the storage unit in use.

The back of the unit

Taking things further

Covered in this chapter

■ Tablecloth and napkins
Dyeing threads and yarns
Enhancing dyed fabrics

■Tablecloth and napkins

Using the techniques described in this book, you can, quite easily, create a unique tablecloth with different coloured napkins. See front cover.

I have given instructions for two ways of dyeing a tablecloth, either in a bag or in a tray. The napkins can be tie-dyed or dyed using the colour mixing method. The directions are for two sizes, but it would be quite simple to change the measurements to suit the table you have in mind.

Equipment and materials

You will need

1 Cat-litter-trays – at least 2 of the same size
2 Dessertspoons and jars for dye solutions
3 Plastic bags
4 Bowl
5 Measuring jug
6 Measuring spoons
7 Cling film
8 Soda solution
9 Salt solution
10 Dye powder in at least 2 colours
11 Fabric – see below

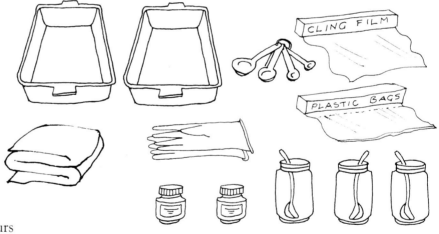

Fabric

Cotton sheeting works well, but linen or a fine lawn could also be used to good effect.

Just remember: whatever is used, it must be 100% natural fibres.

■ For a large tablecloth and 6 napkins, you will need 3.5 metres by 1.5 metres of fabric
■ For a small tablecloth and 6 napkins, you will need 2 metres by 1.5 metres wide, or 3 metres by 1 metre of fabric.

Please note that all directions are given for 150 cm wide cotton sheeting – you may need to adjust amounts for different widths and weights of fabric.

Dyeing the tablecloth – in a tray

I Prepare the fabric

Cut off 1 metre of fabric from the main piece – this will be used to make the napkins.

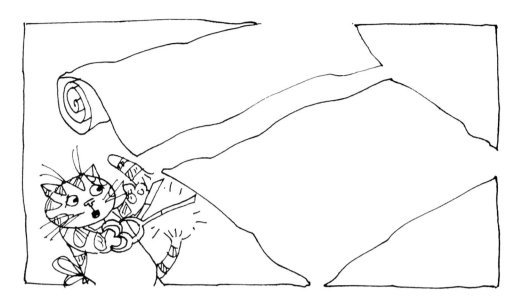

The remaining fabric, to be used for the tablecloth, needs to be soaked in a soda and salt solution for about 30 minutes.

See page 45 for more details.

The soaking solution:

Large tablecloth

> 250 ml (1 cup) soda solution

> 250 ml (1 cup) salt solution

> 1 litre (5 cups) water

Small tablecloth

> 100 ml (⅓ cup) soda solution

> 100 ml (⅓ cup) salt solution

> 500 ml (2 cups) water

❗ Tips

The fabric for the tablecloth can be soaked in advance and allowed to dry if this is more convenient.

---

2 Mix dye solution

For each colour mix ½ teaspoon of dye powder in a jar with:

- 250 ml (1 cup) of water

- a squirt of washing-up liquid to help the dye powder to mix

This makes quite a strong solution. Should you want slightly paler shades, mix with more water.

Prepare two colours – remember to choose primary colours if you want bright results.

For a small tablecloth, one jar of each colour will be sufficient, but for the larger cloth, you will need two jars of each colour.

3 In goes the fabric

Carefully scrunch up your prepared fabric into the cat-litter tray.

Slowly feed in the fabric – remember, the more you twist and tweak, the more interesting the patterns.

4 Spoon on the colours

When all the fabric is in the tray, start to spoon on the colours. Spoon on about half of the mixed dye solution – mixing the colours as you go.

Press down with the back of your hand to blend the colours a little more – try not to leave any white patches.

5 Add more colour

Take the second cat-litter tray and put it, upside down, on top of the first, like a lid. Turn both trays over so the fabric falls neatly into the second tray with the other side up.

Push the fabric down a bit if it needs it. Then spoon on the rest of the dye solution as before.

6 Leave to set

Leave for 24 hours – cover with some cling film or put the whole thing in a plastic bag to prevent the fabric from drying out.

7 Take out and rinse

Take out and rinse, wash and rinse.

See directions in Chapter 6, page 48.

Dyeing the tablecloth – in a bag

1 Prepare the fabric

The first thing you need to do is to prepare the fabric.

Cut off 1 metre of fabric – this will be used to make the napkins. The remaining fabric will be used for the tablecloth.

Tie up the tablecloth fabric using any of the tie-and-dye techniques described in Chapter 4.

Any of these techniques will work, but because you are working with such a large piece of fabric, the folding method is the easiest to do.

2 Prepare the dye bath in a plastic bag

- **Small tablecloth** – 20 dessertspoons dye solution (mix the colour you want from the original pure solutions – see page 11)

  500 ml (2 cups) soda solution

  100 ml (⅓ cup) salt solution

- **Large tablecloth** – 30 dessertspoons dye solution (mix the colour you want from the original pure solutions – see page 11)

  600 ml (2⅓ cups) soda solution

  100 ml (⅓ cup) salt solution

3 Put the fabric into the bag

- Carefully introduce the fabric bundle to the plastic bag.

- Make sure the solution has soaked into all parts of the fabric.

- Tie a knot in the bag.

- Leave for 24 hours to allow time for the dye to really soak into the fabric.

- Remove from the bag, rinse the bundle in cold water, then untie and rinse again.

Wash and rinse the fabric as described in Chapter 6, page 48.

Dyeing the napkins

1 Prepare the fabric

Prepare the fabric by cutting it into 50 cm squares.

2 Mix the dye solution

Mix 2 teaspoons of dye powder with 200 ml of water.

Make up 2 colours in this way. Use the same colours as used for the tablecloth.

In the recipes below, one will be referred to as colour A and the other colour as B.

3 Prepare to dye

The napkins will be dyed using the basic plastic-bag method as described on page 14.

To dye 6 napkins in 6 different but harmonious colour ways, follow the recipes below.

1   5 dessertspoons colour A plus a drip of colour B
2   4 dessertspoons colour A and 1 dessertspoon colour B
3   3 dessertspoons colour A and 2 dessertspoons colour B
4   2 dessertspoons colour A and 3 dessertspoons colour B
5   1 dessertspoons colour A and 4 dessertspoons colour B
6   5 dessertspoons colour B plus a drip of colour A

> **Tips**
> A drip of dye added to napkins 1 and 6 are to tone down the pure colours a little so that they blend in with the other napkins

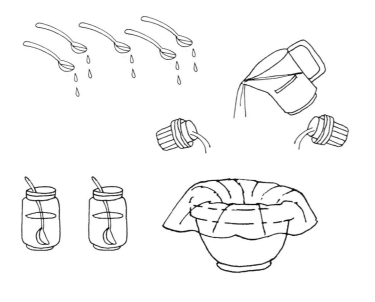

Finishing the tablecloth and the napkins

When all the fabric is washed, rinsed and dried, carefully iron each piece and hem the raw edges.

Variations

- For a stronger effect, the tablecloth which was dyed in the cat-litter tray could be re-dyed using the same technique.

  You will need to complete the process up to the final rinse before starting the whole process over again with a new set of dye solutions. If you intend to use the pre-soaked method, see page 65. The fabric will of course have to be soaked again in the soaking solution before you start.

- The tablecloth that was dyed in the plastic bag could also be re-dyed in a different colour.

  The fabric would need to be retied in a different direction before dyeing again in a contrasting colour.

- The napkins can be tie-dyed using any of the methods described in Chapter 4.

See pictures facing page 31.

Dyeing threads and yarns

Threads and yarns can be dyed for use in embroidery, quite simply, using the cat-litter-tray technique.

The same rules apply:

- Natural fibres work best, such as cotton, silk or linen.
- The dye must be left on the fabric long enough to work.
- Soda must be added at some point to fix the dye.

Equipment and materials

You will need

1 Cat litter trays or something similar
2 Rubber gloves, old clothes, protected surfaces, etc.
3 Measuring spoons
4 Dessert spoons and jars for dye solution
6 Thread – prepared and ready to use – see next page
7 Soda solution
8 Salt solution
9 Dye powder

You will also need

For dyeing machine thread, a jar or a piece of plastic pipe
For dyeing thicker threads, a extendable clothes hanger.

Machine thread

Machine thread can be dyed for use in machine embroidery or to create an exact match for some hand-dyed fabric.

Any of the cat-litter-tray techniques can be used, but I find that the simplest is the second method, where the soda and salt is mixed in with the dye solution.

1 Prepare the thread

The thread must be taken off the reel and wound on to either a glass jar or a piece of plastic pipe. This is to make sure that all the thread is exposed to the dye and not covered. It does sound a bit of a fiddle but it really does not take that long.

The thread must be thoroughly soaked in water after it has been wound – you may find you need to rub it a little to make sure it does get really wet.

2 Dye the thread

Mix up the dye solution.

Lay the thread in a tray and just spoon on the dye. More than one colour can be used to give multi-coloured threads. Roll the pipe or the jar so that all the thread is dyed.

Leave for at least 30 minutes – longer if you can.

Take it out and while the thread is still wrapped on the jar or pipe, rinse in cold water, wash in hot soapy water and then give a final rinse in cold water.

When the thread is completely dry, wind it back on to the reel ready for use.

> **! Tips**
>
> Thread can be dyed to match a piece of fabric by just popping it in the bag with the fabric at the time of dyeing. You will need to transfer the thread from the reel on to a piece of flat plastic so that all the thread is exposed to the dye. A piece of plastic measuring 10 cm (4 in) x 15 cm (6 in) is quite sufficient for 100 metres of thread. I find the plastic sheets used for template making in patchwork are good, but anything will do as long as it is not going to disintegrate in the dye.

Thicker yarn

All sorts of yarn can be dyed as long as it is made from a natural fibre. If you are not sure, do the burn test – see page 8.

Any of the cat-litter-tray techniques can be used, but I find that the simplest is the second method, where the soda and salt is mixed in with the dye solution.

1 Prepare the yarn

The yarn must be wound into hanks so that it is all exposed to the dye solution. There are special wool winders and hank winders on the market but I use an adjustable clothes hanger – the sort you get when you buy a new skirt or pair of trousers.

Just wind the yarn around the hanger, which should be extended to its widest point. Secure the hank by tying small pieces of yarn around the wound threads at intervals – 3 on each side of the hanger will be enough. Don't tie these too tightly or the dye will not be able to penetrate. When the hank is securely tied, reduce the size of the hanger by pushing it in and gently remove the hank.

2 Dye the yarn

Mix up the dye solution.

Lay the hanks of yarn in a tray and just spoon on the dye. More than one colour can be used to give multi-coloured effects. Turn the hanks over to make sure they are evenly dyed.

Leave for at least 30 minutes – longer if you can.

Take out the hanks of yarn and wrap in cling film and leave to set for a couple of hours. They can be left longer if this is more convenient

Remove from the cling film. Rinse in cold water, wash in hot soapy water and rinse again in cold water until the water runs clear. Then hang up to dry.

The yarn can then be wound into balls or used straight from the hank, whichever is easier

> **! Tips**
> Yarn that is made up of a mixture of fibres can give interesting results when dyed. The only real way to find out is to try a piece and see.

> **! Tips**
> Yarn can be dyed using the plastic-bag method if solid-coloured threads are required. The yarn must be wound into hanks and then dyed following the instructions for plastic-bag dyeing in Chapter 2. Yarn and fabric can be dyed in the same bag for matching colours.

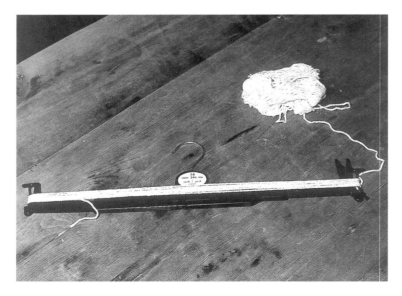

Enhancing dyed fabrics

Fabrics that have been hand dyed make excellent canvases for embroidery.

If you look closely at a piece of space-dyed or tie-and-dyed fabric, it is possible to pick out beautiful patterns and even pictures that can be enhanced with threads.

Random embroidery

Free machine embroidery is a wonderful way to enhance dyed fabric. Just follow the lines and see what appears, and by putting some wadding beneath the fabric, textures can also be developed.

There are many books on the market which cover the techniques of free machine embroidery and I have listed a few on page 78.

Transferring pictures to fabric

In order to embroider a definite picture, you will first need to create your design on paper and then transfer it to the fabric.

The simplest way to do this is with the aid of a light box. The paper is put on the light box and covered with the fabric, and then it is quite easy to trace the design or picture straight onto the fabric. I use a very sharp lead pencil rather than a felt-tip pen. The embroidery will cover the lines and the pencil gives a sharper mark than felt pens.

If you have not got a light box, you can make one by just putting a little lamp under an up-turned pale-coloured plastic crate. Otherwise, just tape the design and fabric to a window and trace.

Embroidering a picture

There are no hard-and-fast rules for this, but one of the most effective ways is to just outline the pictures using free machining techniques. If the fabric has been placed on wadding prior to sewing, the outlining will make the pictures puff up. These can be accentuated even more by filling in the spaces between the pictures with lots of machine embroidery.

See the cot quilt facing page 63.

Couching

Dyed yarns can be used in any couching designs to very good effect. A simple example can be seen facing page 62.

FAQs (Frequently asked questions)

1. Are Procion MX dyes dangerous to use?

Procion MX dyes are not toxic but can cause allergies if not treated with some respect. I would advise the use of a mask when handling dye powder for any length of time. I try and mix my dyes and get them packed away as soon as possible; I feel much happier when I am working with them in solution.

Wear gloves to avoid too much dye on your hands – a little doesn't do any harm.

Keep utensils used for dyeing separate from those used for cooking, and make sure you clean up well after a dyeing session in the kitchen.

I have heard it said that many of the cleaning products used in the kitchen are far more toxic than Procion MX dyes

2. Are cold-water dyes better than the ones you boil?

Procion MX dyes are fibre reactive dyes, which means the dye actually reacts with the fibre and creates a permanent colouring. Dyes which are boiled are direct dyes and are not as permanent and have a greater tendency to 'bleed'.

3. Can I use any fabric?

You will get better results from fabric made from natural fibres – cotton, linen, silk. For strong colours, use 100% natural fibre, but it is possible to get some nice pastels from mixed-fibre fabrics.

4. How do I know if my fabric is 100% cotton?

The simplest test is to cut a small piece of fabric, put it in an old saucer or something similar and burn it. If the smoke is white and the residue is like soft powder, the fabric is 100% natural fibre; if the smoke is black and the residue is sticky or gritty, then there is a percentage of man-made fibre in the fabric.

5. What does 'Mercerised' mean?

Mercerisation means the cotton yarns or fabrics have been treated with a concentrated solution of caustic alkali. This causes the fibres to swell and consequently improve dye affinity, strength, handle and lustre. If the fabric is stretched during this process, the lustre is further enhanced. Mercerised fabric can be more expensive but the dyed results will be stronger and darker.

6. I thought the salt should go in before the soda – does it matter putting them in at the same time?

Absolutely correct – the salt normally goes in first to allow the dye to get out of the water into the fabric before any reaction takes place. The soda causes a reaction and the dye will react with

whatever it is on or in – water, hands, fabric. The reason I put it all in together is pure ease. I do make sure the fabric goes in immediately following the solutions and, so far, I have been satisfied with my results.

As I have said many times, if there is a simple way and it works, why complicate things?

7. I have had problems dissolving the salt.

The salt is quite difficult to dissolve and will not fully disappear unless there are at least 2 litres of water. If you start with one litre of boiling water, this will get it started – but you do need the full two litres to fully dissolve the salt.

Can you remember chemistry lessons on saturated solutions?

8. Can't I use the dye solution that is left in the bag?

This question comes up time and time again. The thing is that although it might look good, the reactive qualities of the dye have ceased and this solution is no good for dyeing fabrics any longer. If, however, you like designing on paper, it does make reasonable coloured ink.

9. Will my fabric be wash fast?

If you have followed the instructions for washing and rinsing correctly, the answer is yes.

If, however, you are a bit worried, there is something on the market called a Dye Magnet – see List of suppliers on page 77. This is put in with the wash and collects any dye that runs before it can do any damage.

10. Will my fabric be light fast?

Yes, under normal conditions. If you display your work in a sunny window for days on end, then no.

The hand-dyed fabrics used in quilts that I have made have retained their colour while commercially dyed fabrics have faded.

11. Will it matter if I leave the fabric in the bag for longer than 3 hours?

If you are using cotton, there is no problem – in fact, I have found the longer the better. I would be a little more careful with silk. The soda solution will start to damage the silk after 3 hours.

12. Must I wash all my fabrics separately?

When dyeing fabrics of different colours, it is better to keep them separate.

I rinse them all on their own and then wash, for example, all the reds together. The next rinse I do separately and then, when the water is running clear, I put the whole lot, different colours together, in the washing machine for a final rinse. Then get them dry as quickly as you can.

13. Is it necessary to iron fabric to fix the colour?

No, the fixing has been done by the soda solution. Ironing, however, does make the fabrics look wonderful. I still get pleasure from seeing a pile of freshly ironed hand-dyed fabrics.

14. Why do I get big white patches on my tie-and-dyed fabrics?

This could be caused by extremely tight tying or by wetting the fabric before dyeing. If you do this, water acts as a resist and will not let the dye penetrate into the fabric. If you tie-dye dry fabric, the dye will 'wick' its way in and you will get wonderful shading of colour and no white spots.

15. Why do I get different colours appearing on my tie-dyed pieces?

This happens when dyes have been mixed. The pigment from the different colours separates out and travels through the fabric at different speeds, giving some wonderful effects.

16. How long will the dye stay on my hands?

No matter how careful you are, you usually get some dye on your hands. This goes within a couple of days. Washing, scrubbing and the application of hand cream all help.

17. Will the dye stain my work tops?

I wouldn't like to take the risk. Protect all work areas with plastic before you start. Although dye does not stain white porcelain sinks, beware of little cracks – it can get into those.

18. How do I get dye out of my clothes?

Dyers Law: Anything you don't want dyed will dye more permanently than anything else!
Wear old clothes, wear an apron and be careful. If an accident does occur, the quicker you can get the article washed, the better.

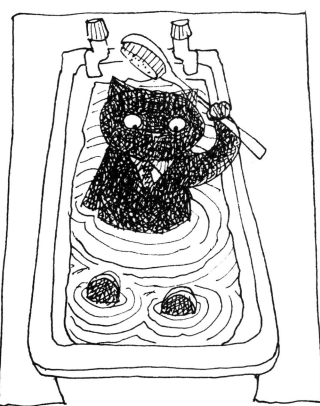

 In an emergency

Eye contact	Immediately irrigate with clean water for at least 15 minutes.
Ingestion	Rinse mouth and drink plenty of water but DO NOT induce vomiting.
Inhalation	Reactive dyes can cause allergies. If symptoms similar to hay fever or asthma occur, seek medical advice.

People suffering from asthma or those with chronic chest disease should avoid handling dyes in powder form.

List of suppliers

Lakeland Limited *for measuring spoons and cups*
Alexandra Buildings
Windermere
Cumbria LA23 1BQ
Tel: 015394 88100
Fax: 015394 88300
Web site: www.lakelandlimited.com

Whaleys (Bradford) Ltd. *for fabric*
Harris Court
Great Horton
Bradford
West Yorkshire BD7 4EQ

Croft Mill *for fabric*
Tel: 01282 869625
Fax: 01282 870038
E-mail: info@croftmill.co.uk

George Weil *for fabric and dye supplies*
Old Portsmouth Road
Peasmarsh
Guildford
Surrey
GU3 1LZ
Tel: 01483 565800
Fax: 01483 565807
E-mail: sales@georgeweil.co.uk

Rainbow Silks *for textile decoration and silk painting supplies (including dyes)*
6 Wheelers Yard, High Street
Great Missenden
Bucks HP16 0AL
Tel: 01494 862111
Fax: 01494 862651
Web site: www.rainbowsilks.co.uk

Kemtex Educational Supplies *for dye supplies*
Chorley Business and Technology Centre
Euxton Lane
Chorley
Lancashire PR7 6TE
Tel: 01257 230220
Fax: 01257 230225
Web site: www.kemtex.co.uk

Vycombe Arts *for dyes*
Fenway
Fenwalk
Woodbridge
Suffolk IP12 4AS
Tel/Fax: 01394 380882

The Quilt Room *for specialist patchwork supplies*
20 West Street
Dorking
Surrey RH4 1BL
Tel: 01306 740739
Mail order – Tel: 01306 877407
Fax: 01306 877407
Web site: www.quiltroom.co.uk

Winifred Cottage *for specialist embroidery supplies*
17 Elms Road
Fleet
Hampshire GU13 9EG
Tel: 01252 617667
E-mail: winifcott@AOL.com
Web sites:
for price list:
www.egroups.com/group/infoAtwinifredcottage
for questions and answers:
www.egroups.com/group/winifredcottage

Useful Web sites

DyersLIST – e-mailing list
To subscribe to the DyersLIST send an e-mail to listproc@list.emich.edu with the following request
Subscribe DyersLIST your name

http://home.flash.net/~pburch/dyeing.html
Paula Burch is an extremely accomplished American dyer and her web site is packed with useful information

www.jacquardproducts.com
– lots of good information for dyers

www.dyesonline.com – as above

www.prochemical.com/store/
– a US company selling dyes and the web site is packed with information

www.dripak.co.uk – information on washing soda

Book list

Colour Theory

Blue and Yellow Don't Make Green *Michael Wilcox* ISBN 0-9587891-9-3

Colour *Zelanski and Fisher* ISBN 0-906969-95-6

The Elements of Colour *Itten* ISBN 0-471-28929-9

Embroidery

Machine Embroidery Stitch Techniques *Valerie Campbell-Harding, Pamela Watts* ISBN 0-7134-5797-X

The Machine Embroiderer's Handbook *Val Holmes* ISBN 0-7134-7983-3

Surface Design

Complex Cloth *Jane Dunnewold* ISBN 1-56477-149-0

Dyeing Techniques

Color By Accident *Ann Johnston* ISBN 0-9656776-0-5

Patchwork Techniques

Discover Patchwork *Tina Ealovega* ISBN 0-600-58591-3

Geometric Patterns from Patchwork Quilts *Robert Field* ISBN 1-899618-41-4

Strip Patchwork *Valerie Campbell-Harding* ISBN 0-7134-1319-0

The Complete Book of Patchwork, Quilting and Appliqué *Linda Seward* ISBN 1-85732-856-6

The Perfect Patchwork Primer *Beth Gutcheon* ISBN 0-14-046-212-0

Workshops and lectures

Contact Helen Deighan for a list of workshops, demonstrations and lectures.
Roseglen
Crossways Road
Grayshott
Hindhead
Surrey GU26 6HG

Glossary

Bowl	A kitchen mixing bowl or pudding basin – approximately 1 litre (2 pint) size
Calico	Plain woven strong cotton cloth (sometimes bleached), with a distinctive fleck in the weave (British definition)
Cling film	Plastic film used for wrapping or covering food – US Glad Wrap
Clothes horse	Structure for airing or drying clothes
Fat quarter	A piece of cloth measuring approximately 50 cm x 50 cm – or 0.5 metre cut in half along a line running parallel to both selvage edges
Fixitol P	A 'fastness booster' – helps to fix dyes as well as preventing contamination in the washing process
Jar	A glass jar that has contained jam (British definition), pickles or mayonnaise – approximately 350 ml or 1½ cup size
Laundry liquid	Liquid used for washing clothes
Laundry magnet	A device for collecting any colour particles that have come out of dyed fabric in the wash. This prevents spoiling other fabrics in the same wash. Looks like a piece of towelling.
Overlocker	A sewing machine which cuts and neatens edges at the same time – also known as a **serger**
Procion	The trade name for fibre reactive dyes made by ICI
Set	The term used for leaving fabric for a period of time in order that the dye has time to thoroughly soak into the fabric
Spoons **Tea**	5 ml spoon used for stirring a cup of tea
Dessert	10 ml spoon used for eating dessert
Table / serving	15 ml spoon used for serving food
Sticky tape	Clear or coloured adhesive tape such as 'Scotch' or 'Sellotape'
Tights	Nylon stockings or panti-hose
Synthrapol	Prevents any loose particles of dye from contaminating other fabrics. Metapex 38 liquid works like Synthrapol
Wadding	Batting or filling used in between or underneath fabric for quilting purposes or to add texture
Washing-up liquid	Liquid used for hand washing plates or dishes
Work surfaces	Table top, unit top or kitchen bench top
Zig-zag stitch	Special stitch, on a swing-needle sewing machine, for neatening edges

Measurements

Conversion table

The amounts listed below are exact measurements which we have rounded up for the recipes used in the book e.g. 1 dessertspoon = 10ml.

Liquid measure

1 teaspoon	⅓ tablespoon	⅙ fluid ounce	4.9 millilitres
2 teaspoons	1 dessertspoon	⅓ fluid ounce	9.8 millilitres
3 teaspoons	1 tablespoon	½ fluid ounce	14.8 millilitres
6 teaspoons / 3 dessertspoons	2 tablespoons	1 fluid ounce	29.6 millilitres
16 teaspoons / 8 dessertspoons	⅓ cup	2 ⅔ fluid ounces	79 millilitres
8 tablespoons	½ cup	4 fluid ounces	118 millilitres
16 tablespoons	1 cup	8 fluid ounces	.237 litre
2 cups	1 pint	16 fluid ounces	.473 litre
2 pints	1 quart	32 fluid ounces	.946 litre
4 quarts	1 gallon	128 fluid ounces	3.785 litre

Solid weight

1 ounce	28.35 grams	
16 ounces	1 pound	453.6 grams
2.2 pounds	1,000 grams	1 kilogram
100 grams	3.5 ounces	
10 grams	.35 ounces	
1 gram	1,000 milligrams	

Metric fluid capacity

10 millilitres	1 centilitre	.338 fluid ounces
100 millilitres	1 decilitre	3.38 fluid ounces
1,000 millilitres	1 litre	1.05 liquid quarts
10 litres		2.64 gallons

Linear measure

1 inch	2.54 centimetres	
1 foot	30.48 centimetres	12 inches
1 yard	.914 metres	3 feet
1 metre	100 centimetres	1.057 yards